Between Struggle and Hope

Between Struggle and Hope

Four Black Educators in the South, 1894–1915

ARNOLD COOPER

Iowa State University Press / Ames

To Belletech, above all

Arnold Cooper teaches at Moorhead State University in Moorhead, Minnesota.

© 1989 Iowa State University Press, Ames, Iowa 50010

Manufactured in the United States of America

First edition, 1989

Library of Congress Cataloging-in-Publication Data

Cooper, Arnold.
    Between struggle and hope.

    Bibliography: p.
    Includes index.
    1. Afro-American teachers—Southern States—Biography. 2. Afro-Americans—Education—Southern States—Case studies. I. Title.
LA2315.S86C66   1989   370′8996073075   88–13705
ISBN 0–8138–0141–9

Contents

Preface

WHEN MONROE N. WORK, DIRECTOR OF Research and Records at Tuskegee Institute, publicized the achievements of graduates in 1911, he noted with pride that twenty-three industrial schools had been "directly or indirectly founded by graduates and former students." These "offshoots" were located in eight southern states and represented a significant extension of the "Spirit of Tuskegee."[1] Educational historians have not studied in depth the replicas of Tuskegee, focusing instead on Booker T. Washington's school or on his alma mater, Hampton Institute. Historian Raymond Gavins has commented on this tendency to single out "men and women of undisputed national reputation, a few black heroes and heroines esteemed the most outstanding representatives of their race . . . [while] lesser known members of the black vanguard remain undeservedly obscure." Gavins calls for studies of "significant minor figures" to provide "new data for the portfolio on how black leaders function."[2]

Whatever became of the "little Tuskegees"? Careful inquiry into the policies and practices of four black southern educators between 1894 and 1915, the year that Washington died, will provide additional data on black educational leadership during the years of Washington's ascendancy. This book seeks to reclaim from the shadow of the Tuskegee principal educators who provided indigenous stewardship for black students in the rural South a generation after emancipation. As members of a significant educational phalanx, these educators established objectives for, and gave direction to, the development of both their students and their communities.

Several major questions need to be addressed in this attempt to shed some light on Tuskegee replicas: What procedures did these educators have to follow in order to establish their schools? Who opposed them? On whom could they rely? What were the societal constraints? What kind of relationship did each school form with its community? What did these schools actually accomplish? And finally, what light does this research shed on the triumphs and travails of Afro-American educational leadership?

This book presents a set of case studies designed to document the development of black education. Historian Elizabeth Jacoway has argued that historians have distorted the study of black industrial education because they have tended "to concentrate on the outcome of the industrial education movement — analyzing the product rather than the process — and often they have read history backwards from the outcome to the intent." Jacoway suggests that a "complete understanding of the industrial education movement must rest first of all on a correct identification and assessment of the assumptions underlying the experience."[3] A basic premise of this study is that by focusing on the evolution of policy and practice, the historian will achieve a balanced view of these schools and their founders.

A portfolio on black educators must also recognize the historical limitations imposed on their leadership. Each educator needs to be etched against his time and place. The agendas and strategies of these men could not be exclusively educational. Political, economic, and racial constraints were always present, constituting a "web of subordination" imposed by whites to dominate and emasculate black educational advancement.[4] A recognition of these constraints and an analysis of the tactics employed to circumvent them are prerequisites for a judicious interpretation of the black educational leaders in this study.

Since the process by which educational ideas were translated into institutions is central to this study, the subjects were selected because they were actual practitioners of industrial education in the South. However, because the scope of this study is confined to four black male educators, no attempt has been made to paint a portrait of a "typical" black educator of the period. In an effort to present a balanced view of process and practice, each case study includes a sketch of the school founder, the compelling circumstances surrounding the establishment of the school, and information concerning the setting and the political and racial factors that existed at the time. Documentation of the development of six features of each school—students, alumni, curriculum, faculty, extension, and fund-raising—is also provided.

A chapter in this study is devoted to each educator. Chapter 1, " 'Deeds Not Words': William J. Edwards and Snow Hill Institute, 1894–1915," concerns a graduate of Tuskegee Institute who founded one of its earliest offshoots in 1894. An examination of the practices of another Tuskegee graduate is offered in Chapter 2, " 'We Rise Upon the Structure We Ourselves Have Builded': William H. Holtzclaw and Utica Institute, 1903–1915." Utica, the only school of its kind organized by a Tuskegee graduate in Mississippi between 1903 and 1915, was an important outpost of Washington's influence. Tuskegee graduates were the subjects of considerable scrutiny by their alma mater. In Chapter 3, "The Tuskegee Machine in Action," Washington's relationships with Edwards and Holtzclaw and his impact on their educational practices are explored.

A black educator who was neither born nor educated in the South is discussed in Chapter 4, " 'Lighting a Pine Torch': Laurence C. Jones and the Piney Woods Country Life School, 1909–1915." Jones, a native of Missouri, was a liberal arts graduate of the University of Iowa who left the Midwest for Mississippi. He worked at Utica Institute with Holtzclaw for two years before he started his own school in a neighboring county. The ideas and methods of another educator with a collegiate liberal arts background are analyzed in Chapter 5, " 'An Educator and an Humble Christian Worker': Thomas O. Fuller and Howe Institute, 1900–1915." Fuller, a theology graduate of Shaw University in Raleigh, North Carolina, founded two Baptist schools in the 1890s and served a term in the North Carolina Senate before he moved to Memphis in 1900. Two years later he became the principal of Howe Institute, a Baptist school on the brink of closing. Fuller is the only educator in this study who worked in an urban setting, and his experiences as a school builder reflected the manner in which the Tuskegee model could find expression in the city.

Acknowledgments

MANY PEOPLE HELPED in the completion of this study. George A. Kizer made it possible in the first place because of his guidance and encouragement. Other Iowa State University mentors include Charles R. Kniker, Clair Keller, Helen H. Schuster, and William A. Hunter. The Interlibrary Loan Staff at Iowa State helped immeasurably. I received inspiration from the work of Alferdteen Harrison and V. P. Franklin. Elaine Schmidt and Karen Vosburgh diligently and competently typed numerous drafts. Throughout my travels and residence in the South, I have been privileged to share trust and faith with the Dillards of Newellton, Louisiana; the Brantleys of Ridgeland, South Carolina; and Nina Blount and the Elberts of Winterville, North Carolina. All of these people have fought for educational equity in an environment that any of the four educators in this study would have understood all too well. My greatest debt is to my wife, Belletech Deressa, whose tenderness and thoughtfulness have sustained me. Her contributions are so numerous that to repay them would surely bankrupt my heart. This book is dedicated to her with love.

Between Struggle and Hope

Chapter One

"Deeds Not Words"

William J. Edwards
and Snow Hill Institute, 1894–1915

ONE OF THE MOST SIGNIFICANT MEMBERS OF TUSKEGEE Institute's educational phalanx was William J. Edwards, founder of Snow Hill Institute in Wilcox County, Alabama, in the western part of Alabama's Black Belt. Robert Sherer maintains that Snow Hill was "the most successful of the offshoots of Tuskegee in Alabama, both in its achievements and in the hardships which its founder had to overcome." Joseph Citro analyzed Tuskegee's monthly publication, the *Southern Letter,* and discovered that between 1885 and 1912 Edwards was one of seven graduates repeatedly singled out and praised for his efforts at spreading the Tuskegee gospel.[1] Edwards also has the distinction of being one of the earliest founders of a Tuskegee offshoot, having started his school in 1894, only five years after Cornelia Brown had established the first offshoot, Mt. Meigs Colored Institute at Waugh, Alabama.[2]

Edwards was born on September 12, 1869, in the Black Belt community of Snow Hill, three-quarters of a mile east of where he was to build his school twenty-five years later. He was an orphan at the age of six. The task of rearing Edwards was left to his paternal grandmother and eventually to an aunt. At the age of twelve Edwards became ill from scrofula, a bone disease that affected his legs and caused him to walk only with much difficulty and pain. He was operated on in 1884 and regained his ability to walk three years later.[3] Overall, Edwards's childhood was marked by hunger and deprivation:

Sometimes I would go to school for weeks with nothing to eat but a

3

little corn bread that had nothing in it but salt and water. And, too, my feet would become so chapped by going to school in the cold without shoes that, when I would wash them at night, they would bleed. The pain would be so great at times I would cry for hours.[4]

Edwards heard about Tuskegee Institute while attending a church revival in 1887. He rented several acres of land, raised a crop, and used the proceeds to enter the school in 1889. Four years later he graduated second in a class of twenty. His class motto was "Deeds Not Words." Booker T. Washington had a profound influence on Edwards, who remembered the Tuskegee founder's Sunday evening talks stressing the need for service to black people: "I could understand every word he said, and too, I felt always that he was talking directly to me."[5] The vision of duty to the unfortunate that Washington had placed before him decided Edwards's lifework. Snow Hill, the place of his boyhood struggles, was to be his proving ground, and graduation from Tuskegee conferred on him "almost an ordination as a minister of the Tuskegee gospel."[6]

Aspiration did not translate easily into acceptance. When Edwards returned home in the summer of 1893, he began teaching summer school in an "old dilapidated log cabin . . . they were using for a school house" despite being cursed with "many oaths" by the chairman of the local white school trustees. He also used the summer months to learn the "real condition of our people" by travelling 157 miles through four neighboring counties. Edwards drew a stark portrait of blacks: he found the "religious and moral condition of the people very low . . . with little regard for truth and none at all for promises. . . . Their homes were usually one-room log cabins, which were often kept quite dirty and filthy."[7]

His discoveries on this journey convinced Edwards to build a school and also determined its character. He moved cautiously, however. Conditions differed greatly from those surrounding the establishment of Tuskegee Institute. No political collaboration between blacks and whites existed in Wilcox County, and Edwards received no telegram inviting him to become principal, as had his mentor.[8] Instead, the recent normal school graduate felt the need to canvass contiguous counties in order to be sure of his ground. In the spring of 1894, he called several black men together ("all unlettered but one") and proposed the idea of an industrial school, "to make education practical rather than theoretical."[9]

But Edwards could not easily translate his vision into reality. He had to contend with many black parents who opposed his "industrial plank" with the objection that "the end of education was to free their children from manual labor rather than prepare them for more and better work." Teachers "here and there who had not attended any Industrial School" and "illiterate preachers . . . who had not had any particular training" led the opposition.[10]

As the school began, Snow Hill Institute also battled to remain free of religious ties. Edwards's own African Methodist Episcopal Church wanted him "to teach a denominational school." When he refused, his minister decided to establish a church school in Snow Hill and offered Edwards the principalship. Church officials threatened "to crush [him] out of existence" if he resisted. He refused to comply because, as he insisted, he was "working for the people and not a certain class."[11] (In contrast to this crisis in Snow Hill, Washington initially benefited from the willingness of a local black church to provide space for his school on its property.[12]) Despite his church's opposition, Edwards started his school in the fall of 1894 with three students, two 20 × 15 recitation rooms, and "without any church or society responsible for one dollar of its expenses."[13]

The development of Snow Hill Institute was no easy task. In 1896, two years after he started his school, he informed Washington of the toll that building the school had taken on him:

I am having a hard time, knowing that, I have no certain source from which to obtain means to carry on this work. . . . Sometimes I get weak and at such times the work suffers. . . . I have not had one week's rest since July 1895. . . . No one knows the sacrifice but God. . . . Sometimes I think the end is near but I go struggling on hoping for better times.[14]

The difficulties in keeping a black industrial school financially viable continually plagued Edwards: "We . . . watch with the greatest anxiety each passing month; and when the end is reached even with the least amount of success, it brings to us unspeakable and inexpressible joy; which no one but him upon whom such a burden is placed . . . can wholly appreciate."[15]

Financial support came principally from northern contributors. Edwards traveled with the Tuskegee Institute Quartet when it went north in the summer of 1898 to raise money. This "Northern Campaign" enabled the Snow Hill principal to meet potential donors, especially in Boston, and resulted in yearly trips thereafter. Edwards also formed the Snow Hill Singers to help raise funds.[16]

As he built his school, Edwards also had to contend with racial tensions and political and educational inequities in Alabama. Between 1893 and 1915, 120 blacks were lynched in the state, including 3 in Wilcox County and 19 in contiguous counties.[17] A school law of 1891 granted local school authorities complete control over the distribution of state funds to black and white schools. The results of this law were illustrated by public school expenditures in Wilcox County. Money spent in 1889–90 amounted to $1.02 per white student and ninety cents per black student. The per capita expense for white students reached $27.75 in 1911–12, while only fifty-four cents was spent to educate a black child. In addition, the average length of the public school term was 6.7 months for whites and only 3.9 months for blacks. These inequities took their toll. By 1910 black illiteracy in Wilcox county reached 50.4 percent, while only 4.4 percent of the white residents could not read and write.[18] Blacks lost not only educational benefits but also their right to vote. The new Alabama Constitution of 1901 disenfranchised black people and enfeebled any political efforts to protest disparities in education.

As a black educator, Edwards noted that "in order for us to do any work at all in the South, we must have the support of the southern white man."[19] He furthered his ambitions through a personal relationship with Randall O. Simpson, a former slaveholder and a Confederate veteran, who owned most of the land around Snow Hill Institute.[20] Edwards was raised on Simpson's plantation, had received money from him when he was sick, and even borrowed money from him to purchase a suit for his Tuskegee commencement. Impressed by what he perceived education had done for Edwards, Simpson gave him seven acres of land in 1894 and encouraged Edwards to build a school that the black laborers on his plantation could attend.[21]

The realities of black educational leadership in the racially circumscribed environment of Wilcox County reinforced Edwards's reliance upon Simpson. The Confederate veteran chaired Snow Hill Institute's Board of Trustees, and his son served as both treasurer and auditor. When Edwards battled his own church for independence in 1894, Simpson's offer of land provided him with the "foundation . . . to go on with my work."[22] Washington extolled the Edwards-Simpson relationship: "No man could watch over a member of his own family with more solicitude and tender care than does Mr. Simpson guard this school, and between him and Edwards there is complete faith." Edwards did not disagree. He called his main white supporter "one of the noblest men that I have ever met. . . . Without R. O. Simpson there could not have been any Snow Hill Institute. We might have built a similar school elsewhere, but we could not have built it at Snow Hill."[23]

Simpson's paternalism had limits, however. He sold 1,400 acres of land to Edwards for twenty-six thousand dollars in 1908, a debt that exacerbated the financial woes of Snow Hill Institute. His donations were occasional. He was "not really in full agreement with the idea of negro-white equality; he fell short of committing himself to . . . [a] more complete negro-white equalitarianism."[24] Nor did he raise any vocal objections to the educational inequities that affected black students.

Washington encouraged Edwards to maintain friendly relationships with other local whites. In 1914 he urged his protégé to make a "stronger and more systematic effort to bring the white people of Wilcox County into close contact with your work. . . . You are not close enough in cooperation with them and do not get hold of the white people in your county in the way that it is possible to do." Edwards admitted his estrangement from local whites. "The white people of the county, for the most part," he said, were "far behind the white people in many other counties of the state [and were] indeed backward in expressing [sup-

8

port]." After twenty years as principal, Edwards forecasted that "altho it will take time, I believe there will be a more cordial cooperation between the white people of the county and the school."[25]

Edwards never permitted his close relationship with Simpson to blind him to the stark realities of his environment. He deliberately selected a school site "1½ mile west of the town [of Snow Hill] . . . [with] not a white family . . . 1½ mile of the place," and criticized the proposed location of his church's rival school for being "in the heart of the village [of Snow Hill] and surrounded by members of the white race which prevents an outlet of any kind." The location of Snow Hill Institute became a recruiting tool, reflecting separateness as well as self-reliance. Nearly every school catalog and annual report repeatedly stated that "we are located in the center of the colored population of this state."[26]

Edwards deliberately promoted the separatist nature of his school's location in letters to potential donors, citing his "dark and benighted" campus and billing it as a "light in the Black Belt." A black visitor to Snow Hill in 1906 also commented that the "chief element of this Institution's importance is, of course, derived from its location: it is right in the midst of the real thing of the American negro race."[27] Wilcox County, indeed, had a black majority. In 1890, four years before Snow Hill Institute was established, blacks comprised 78 percent of the population. By 1910 the black population had reached 82 prcent.[28]

Choosing a school site away from the eyes of white people and solemnizing his predominantly black environment were strategies consciously embraced by Edwards. Indeed, the Snow Hill educator contended that segregation enabled his people to develop self-reliance and independence. Blacks could take advantage of the "benefits wrought by hardship" by establishing their own schools and churches in their own communities.[29]

Edwards publicly ignored southern racism while residing in the South, chooosing to carry a message of dissent to northern audiences only. He criticized educational inequities on fund-raising missions and in promotional literature. For example, he told a group in Lake Placid, New York, that he was "compelled" to seek northern financial support because Southerners were not "educated sufficiently to care for their own problems." Brochures and "Dear friend" letters to northern contributors often highlighted the "plague of ignorance" descending on black people who were "wholly neglected in educational matters." Racism ravaged his people: "Hundreds are being lynched, thousands are being imprisoned, and hurried to premature graves. . . . Racial prejudice still blinds the Southern white . . . from doing the fair, [and] the necessary thing for [the] negro."[30]

Edwards was a modern realist of the first order. He knew that education for blacks in Alabama revolved around issues of race. Since he could not rely upon local white support, he sought "strong Northern men [to be] of some service . . . in getting up the necessary means to carry on this work."[31] He had to be a muted trumpet on race issues in the South but also sound a clarion call for industrial education.

Snow Hill Ideology: Regeneration, Reformation, and Ruralism

Snow Hill Institute's pedagogical framework originated in several recurrent themes articulated by Edwards as he traversed his closed Black Belt society. The idea of change was a fundamental part of his educational philosophy. He believed that blacks in Wilcox County were "starving mentally, morally, religiously and industrially" and that "if not properly fed along these lines, [they] will surely die." Education was the "cure for all of our ills"; as a Tuskegee graduate he came "preaching the gospel of service." Snow Hill Institute, therefore, would "train men and women to be good workers, good leaders, good husbands, good wives, and . . . proper subjects for the kingdom of God."[32]

Edwards envisioned himself as a missionary and a liberator; he intended to train a cadre of students to help rectify the moral and social ills of his people. The ideal Snow Hill graduate would "influence the people to stop living in rented one-room log-cabins," arouse "educational interest," and promote "good character building." In Edwards's view, black people were not irrevocably chained to their social status. He believed that they could become "better men and better women" and lead "pure and upright lives" because intuitively they knew that education was the "source of all we have and the spring of all our future joys."[33]

Students at Snow Hill Institute endured a strict social regimen. Rules and regulations in the school catalog included prohibitions against "profane language, use of tobacco, intoxicants, card playing and the use of fire arms." All students were expected to be "neat of work and clean of person." The school's location contributed to a proper moral environment because "NO SALOONS ARE NEAR."[34]

Religious training was not neglected. Although Edwards had battled to keep his school nondenominational, he wanted to develop Christian character in his pupils. His school had its own chaplain, and the *Bible* was studied as "History, Ethics, and Religion," with prayer meetings every Friday evening. Residential students followed a rigorous routine on Sundays: "Students attended a Y.M.C.A. Meeting at 9:00 a.m., preaching services in the chapel at 11:00 a.m., and Sunday School classes immediately [afterward]." The whole school assembled in the chapel for an evening service conducted by Edwards.[35] In 1913 the school offered a *Bible* course for ministers. Edwards believed that black people needed an "educated and moral ministry . . . properly fitted for their work," and he cynically referred to illiterate black preachers whose "texts were as often taken from Webster's blue-backed-speller as from the *Bible,* and sometimes this would be held upside down."[36]

In Edwards's view, the moral, educational, and social regeneration of black people could only be accomplished in the rural South. Edwards claimed that agriculture and black landownership comprised the "basis" of his work. He intended to "inculcate in [our] students a real love for [the] country life [by] educating the negro to be a skillful farmer and settling him upon small farms of his own." Snow Hill Institute frequently advertised that it was located in an area where "ninety-nine percent of the people . . . depend upon some form of agriculture for a livelihood." The message was clear: "It is our aim to make this primarily an agricultural school, and thus fit these people for their life's work."[37]

Black Belt ruralism offered Edwards's constituency the "opportunity of the age." Although many of his brethren were leaving Wilcox County, the Snow Hill principal argued that "in spite of the denial of political rights . . . of poor educational opportunities and many other unjust discriminations, the South . . . is the best place in this country for the Negro." Edwards did not want black people to go North or to move to southern cities. His commitment to agrarianism was not meant to be self-serving. He believed that black people had a "better opportunity [to develop] a solid and enduring character" in the rural South."[38]

Like many other black educators in the "Tuskegee Circle," Edwards embraced the "doctrine of permanence," which stipulated that blacks should remain southern agrarians forever. He never departed from this belief. In the twilight of his principalship, he made the following plaint:

Too many of our young men and women have no vision as to the future, they want to go thru school and run off to Chicago, Detroit, N.Y. and other large cities and do mere work that any ordinary man can do. We are not educating you for that, but here in the South a great work is before us, and the vast majority of our people are here.[39]

Edwards embraced community extension services as a key objective for the school. He wanted to establish "in the minds of the people of this section the fact that the South is the best place for the Negro."[40] To accomplish this goal, Edwards established three important community services: the Snow Hill Farmers' Conference, an annual gathering at which farmers could receive "new ideas, new information, and [could] take fresh courage"; the Workers' Conference for "teachers and preachers [to present] what [they] are doing, the methods they are pursuing, and the results being achieved"; and the Black Belt Improvement Society, a community organization designed to "reach the ills that most retard the negroes of the South."[41] The Society formed various committees that met each month. For example, the education committee encouraged blacks in Wilcox County "to build better schoolhouses, to extend school terms, and to keep their children in school." The labor committee was formed "to gather together those of our race who still work as contract-hands . . . day-laborers, and domestics [sic] servants, and impress upon them the necessity of rendering their best service."[42] The purpose of these activities was to promote self-sufficiency and to improve living conditions.

Edwards started his school with 3 students in 1894. Four years later a school catalog listed a student body of 186. An analysis of enrollment data reveals that the average annual student count for the period 1902–15 was 319. Female students consistently outnumbered male students, but the differences were not overwhelming.[43] Students in the Training School (the first through sixth grades) comprised 77 percent of the entire student body by 1908. A student had to be at least fourteen years old to enter the two-year teacher training program or to learn a trade. Normal school students never exceeded 23 percent of the enrollment between 1902 and 1915.[44]

Only a very small percentage of students who attended Snow Hill Institute actually graduated with a normal school diploma or a trade certificate. Edwards stated in 1905 that his school only had thirty-seven "official" graduates and "about five hundred others [who] have been under the influence of the school for a longer or shorter period." In 1910, after sixteen years' work, Snow Hill informed the United States Commissioner of Labor that "80 percent of the pupils never graduate. . . . Many leave school for the purpose of earning their own living."[45]

An analysis of the status of Snow Hill alumni helps to reveal the school's legacy. Between 1899 and 1915, 38 percent of all normal school graduates with identifiable employment were teachers. Snow Hill Institute employed 29 percent of this group, 44 percent taught in Alabama, and 26 percent left the state to teach in other southern states. Twenty percent of all normal school alumni moved from the South. It is clear that Edwards could not stem the migration of his teacher-graduates from the Black Belt. But once they left the state their employment opportunities in public schools were evidently limited. For example, seven of the nine graduates who taught in other southern states did so only in two private black industrial schools similar to Snow Hill Institute.[46]

Fifty-one students received a trade certificate from Snow

Hill between 1899 and 1915. Although Edwards claimed that agriculture was the main feature of his school, a mere 18 percent earned a certificate in farming. Forty-one percent of the industrial education graduates received certificates in cooking, sewing, and laundering, and another 22 percent earned certification in carpentry, blacksmithing, and brickmasonry. Like their normal school counterparts, industrial students departed the Alabama Black Belt. Twenty-one percent moved to other southern states, and another 18 percent migrated North.[47]

Edwards reported that his aim "from the outset" was to establish an "industrial institution which would give to the masses a thorough English education." Although he insisted that black people needed manual training, his school consistently advertised its "special effort" to train teachers. Normal school students were offered an array of academic subjects, from ancient history to mental and moral philosophy. This academic preparation had a distinct community focus. The "proper use of the English language" was stressed, because "environed as we are" prospective teachers needed to practice "the principles and rules of Grammar and Rhetoric." Moral philosophy included "the interpretation of general ethical knowledge in terms of the conditions immediately surrounding [us]," a veiled reference to community mores and perhaps even to prevailing race relations. Black history was not neglected, either. Students were required to read *The Autobiography of Frederick Douglass* as an example of the "remarkable progress made . . . by the Negro since Emancipation . . . [because] we [realize] that many of his achievements are worthy of consideration by . . . Negro youth."[48]

There is scant information on how effectively Snow Hill conducted its scholastic program. Three Tuskegee staff members who visited the school in 1910 described the teaching of academics as "poor," "in the abstract," and "confined strictly to the book." In addition, they observed that "in some instances the student did not seem to get hold of the subject." Several of the courses failed the test of practicality: "More stress we think should be put upon the things which the students come in daily contact with, in the home, at the school, and in their community, and from these known things, branch off to others. The student then has a thorough foundation and something on which to build."[49]

Edwards's responses to this criticism are not extant, but given his views on education, his school's academic offerings should not be surprising. He regarded education as a means of "character building." Snow Hill sought to prepare its future teachers "to go into the communities where they propose to work and by precept . . . encourage the people to build better schoolhouses and lengthen the school term . . . [and] bring about the needed reform that is so essential to economic and upright living." Whenever his normal school students passed the county teacher's exam, he proudly reported that success to Washington. Edwards wanted no educational limits placed upon black people because segregation compelled them to have "[their] own teachers, preachers, lawyers, doctors, pharmacists, and . . . therefore they should be given the highest and best education that is obtainable."[50] Although prospective teachers at Snow Hill comprised a distinct minority of the student body, Edwards avidly embraced the "normal" descriptor of his institution.

The heart of Snow Hill Institute was its emphasis on agricultural and manual training. Edwards passionately supported industrial education: "If I could, I would write, in letters of gold, the words 'Industrial Education' on every school, every church, and every home in the land." Each course had a definable community and vocational component. Cooking was introduced into the curriculum not only to provide employment for female students but to enable "the girls here to know what is and what is not nutritious . . . [because] we have long since realized that many of the undergrown and weak, unhealthy people in the country, are made so by the food they eat." In Edwards's view, housekeeping would help students distinguish between "the difference in a home and a house," sawmilling would enable the surrounding black community to erect "more neat and comfortable cottages," and farming would prepare students "to go into these dark [black] places and show the people what is best to plant."[51]

Advocacy and adequacy rarely matched, however. Edwards noted in 1903 that his carpentry shop failed "to meet its needs

. . . relative to room and productiveness" and admitted little improvement eight years later. Although he wanted all learning to "revolve around the agriculture department as a centre," he acknowledged that success was elusive because of a lack of funds "to equip this department adequately." After eighteen years' work, the Snow Hill principal admitted that the "industrial work has not been so satisfactory."[52]

He was not his own worst critic. The three Tuskegee visitors in 1910 lambasted Snow Hill's training programs. The carpentry division, they complained, had no machinery, and much of the work presented an "unfinished appearance"; basketry classes suffered because "not very much practical work has been done"; and the cooking classes failed to provide "enough practice." The sawmill was located three miles away and was operated by hired workers rather than students. Agricultural training was especially criticized. The school's barn was not completed, and most of the land went uncultivated. In conclusion, the Tuskegee committee recommended that "more stress be put upon the importance of regular and systematic teaching of industrial classes."[53]

Although the committee from Tuskegee attacked the viability of Snow Hill's instructional program, its appraisal of the faculty was positive: "It appears to us . . . that the teachers had a grasp on the subject taught. . . . We think most of the teachers are in earnest and are doing good work and desire to help the students in every way possible."[54] Thirteen of the thirty-three faculty members were Tuskegee graduates, and two others graduated from Hampton Institute, Washington's alma mater. Nine teachers were Snow Hill graduates, and the remainder came from various historically black schools in the South. Tuskegee remained the prime source for Edwards's staff throughout this period, and this fact may account for the firm endorsement by the visiting committee.

At Washington's request, Robert E. Park, a white sociologist and ghostwriter for the Tuskegee principal, toured fifteen "Tuskegee Schools" and reported his findings in 1913. According to Park, the farm at Snow Hill was "a disgrace" that "unless improved may cause irreparable harm to the reputation of other schools." Several months after the Park report, Washington criticized Edwards for not giving "enough attention to the growing of the ordinary farm and garden crops." The Snow Hill principal admitted that his school had to import vegetables, but he blamed his farm manager, "who knew less and did less than any man we had ever had."[55]

In his efforts to devise an educational program for blacks in the post-Reconstruction Black Belt environment, Edwards began his work under discouraging conditions. The racial stress of the time, the deficient educational background of the black people in his community, the opposition of his church, and the need to build a school from the ground up without visible means to do so, were some of the problems facing the twenty-four-year-old educator when he graduated from Tuskegee Institute in 1893. Furthermore, Edwards inaugurated his work only after he had made an intensive survey of life in rural Alabama.

Yet even though Edwards was committed to the survival of blacks in the rural South and conceived his school as an opportunity for service, rhetoric and reality were not congruent. He celebrated agriculture, but his school's farm failed. Snow Hill had few graduates, and many of them migrated to other southern states or went north. And while he vigorously advocated industrial education, the Snow Hill principal also acknowledged the deficiencies of his own educational offerings. However, in Robert E. Park's opinion, Edwards was an "apparent failure" not because he lacked "the right spirit" but because he "[had] not been able to put [his school] on a secure footing or make of [it] what [he] hoped to do."[56]

Edwards built his school on hope. He wanted his institution to light fires of aspiration, not snuff them out. He sustained a strength and resilience that allowed him to confront an otherwise socially inscribed and historically constituted racial environment by embracing a separatist, self-help philosophy. He viewed industrial education as a rational choice for black educational leadership, but he did not produce as many tangible benefits as he had hoped to produce. A herald for his cause, Edwards dedicated himself "unreservedly to these people, among whom I was reared, among whom I shall continue to labor, and among whom I shall at the last be buried."[57]

SNOW HILL INSTITUTE AFTER 1915: William Edwards
resigned as Snow Hill's principal for reasons of
health in 1924. He died in 1950 at the age of eighty-
one. Snow Hill Institute became a public school in
1936 and closed in 1973 as a result of the desegrega-
tion of schools in Wilcox County.

Chapter Two

"We Rise Upon the Structure We Ourselves Have Builded"

*William H. Holtzclaw
and Utica Institute, 1903–1915*

W ILLIAM H. HOLTZCLAW, ANOTHER progeny of Tuskegee Institute, founded Utica Normal and Industrial Institute in 1903, the first such school established by one of Booker T. Washington's students in the state of Mississippi. Holtzclaw was born to ex-slave parents on June 20, 1870, in Roanoke, Alabama, about fifty miles northeast of Tuskegee. His birth took place on a Sunday afternoon in a "little cabin fourteen feet by sixteen feet, made of split pine poles, with only dirt for a floor."[1] He was the seventh of fifteen children. Holtzclaw (unlike William Edwards, an orphan at the age of six) was raised by both his parents. His father was a sharecropper and his mother a cook for their landlord's family. Although his parents tried to provide the basic needs, deprivation and poverty were always present.

Holtzclaw, a regular field hand at the age of nine, rotated with his brother in attending school: "One day I plowed and he went to school and the next day he plowed and I went to school. In this way we each got a month of schooling in a year." A month of schooling a year had its consequences for Holtzclaw. He lived in a world of ignorance. He recounted an incident when he needed a book on U.S. history, but "I did not then know what was meant by the United States, or by the word history, and my teacher did not tell me even that the land I lived in was the United States."[2]

In 1899, at the age of nineteen, Holtzclaw left home to work for a white couple who lived a few miles away. They gave him thirty-five cents a day and board. While working for this couple, he came across a paper published by Tuskegee and found this invitation: "There is an opportunity for a few able-bodied young men to make their way through school provided they are willing to work. Applications should be made to Booker T. Washington, Principal." Holtzclaw then "scribbled up some sort of application and addressed it simply to 'Booker T. Washington' with nothing else on the envelope. All the same I was admitted."[3]

Holtzclaw's first moments at Tuskegee were somewhat traumatic. When he entered the school in 1890, he took an entrance examination, but as he later recounted, "I could not tell . . . in what county I lived, nor what state, nor what country. I knew that I was from Roanoke, and to me Roanoke was the whole thing."[4] With such a background he was admitted to the second year of the preparatory program, and because he could not afford to pay room and board, he worked on the school farm in addition to attending classes.

When his father died in 1893, Holtzclaw left Tuskegee to help support his mother. He taught for three years in Georgia at a salary of ten dollars a month. His first teaching position provided him with an opportunity to practice the self-reliance he had learned: "I think . . . that I did the people in that community some good, I made them whitewash their fences and clean up their houses and premises."[5] Holtzclaw returned to Tuskegee in 1896, worked as an office boy for Washington, learned the printer's trade, and graduated in 1898. Holtzclaw, like Edwards before him, responded to Washington's "constant advice to us . . . that after leaving school we should go into one of the remote rural districts where [we] were most needed, and teach."[6] Inspired by his class motto, "We Rise Upon the Structure We Ourselves Have Builded," he "determined to go to Mississippi, which to my mind was the darkest section of the South for a colored man."[7]

While debating exactly how he would achieve his goal,

Holtzclaw contacted Edwards, who had graduated from Tuskegee five years earlier, in 1893, and had founded Snow Hill Institute a year later. Holtzclaw informed Edwards of his plans "to go to Mississippi, and try to do what he was doing in the southern part of Alabama." Edwards offered Holtzclaw a position as a teacher of printing. He accepted and stayed four years (1898–1902), while "never losing sight of my Mississippi object."[8]

In the fall of 1899 he went to Mississippi, but he could not find a teaching position. He returned to Snow Hill in January 1900, visited Mississippi again in the fall of that year, failed to find employment as a teacher, and again went back to Snow Hill.[9] He tried for a third time in 1901 without success and decided to settle in Snow Hill. He married Mary Ella Patterson, a Tuskegee graduate, who was in charge of the Women's Department at Snow Hill. Holtzclaw, however, never lost his desire to start a school in Mississippi, and in 1902 he decided to go to Mississippi for the last time: "I resolved that I would go to Mississippi and that nothing but death should come between me and the fulfillment of my purpose."[10] Before he left Snow Hill, one of Holtzclaw's former teachers at Tuskegee visited him, inquired about his intentions, and said, "You know there is no God in Mississippi." Holtzclaw, determined to leave, replied "that I would take the one that Alabama had with me."[11]

Holtzclaw's decision to leave Alabama was carefully plotted. He acknowledged the assistance of the Reverend R. C. Bedford, a white confidant of Washington who often traveled on behalf of the Tuskegee principal to inspect the schools founded by Tuskegee graduates. In 1901, a year before Holtzclaw finally left for Mississippi, he informed Bedford of his plans. Bedford promptly examined "the conditions there before he would permit me to undertake work in Mississippi."[12] Holtzclaw also asked Washington for a recommendation in July 1902, on a trip to Mississippi, and mentioned that he planned to visit the state superintendent of education.[13] Spreading the Tuskegee gospel in another state required planning.

Although Holtzclaw had staked out his territory, he encountered immediate obstacles. When he arrived in Mississippi in the fall of 1902, he "had it in mind that probably I should attempt to start a school at Mound Bayou or somewhere else in

Bolivar County," in the rich cotton lands of the Mississippi Delta where mostly black people lived. He received no encouragement. A white planter told him: "I think it would do harm. What I want here is Negroes who can make cotton and they don't need education to help them make cotton. I could not use educated Negroes on my place."[14] The black founder of Mound Bayou, Isaiah T. Montgomery, also refused his support, because Holtzclaw had no financial backing. A self-described "stranger amidst strange surroundings" with "[my] motives questioned on the one had, and [my] ability to accomplish [my] object on the other," Holtzclaw continued to tour the Delta much like Edwards did in the Alabama Black Belt, but planters would not permit him to start a school on their land.[15]

Holtzclaw therefore decided to try the hill country. He reached the town of Utica (Hinds County) in October and boarded with A. C. Carter, the head deacon of a local black Baptist church. Carter got Holtzclaw an "audience" with the white town counselors, who had recently established a separate school for white students and who recognized that "something had to be done for the few colored children who lived within the corporate limits." They agreed to pay Holtzclaw twenty dollars a month to teach the black pupils of the community and serve as principal of an elementary school.[16]

Strong local black support enabled Holtzclaw to gain access to white authorities. Deacon Carter was an influential figure who "usually made and unmade . . . the teachers in [the] community."[17] Holtzclaw benefited significantly from his association with this local black authority figure in a way not available to Edwards when he established his school in Snow Hill.

Although Holtzclaw taught public school, he immediately began "to agitate the question of an independent school." Private education for blacks in Hinds County was not unusual when he arrived. There were at least two black private elementary schools and four private secondary schools operated by various religious denominations, but none were located in Utica.[18] Holtzclaw wanted to start his own school free of "all entanglements," and his stint at the public school enabled him to "prepare the way" for Utica Institute.[19] But black people were wary of his motives, because "a short while before a trickster had been to the town begging to build a school for his 'needy brethren' and the next thing the donors knew he had a thriving grocery in another town."[20] Holtzclaw persisted, however, and went "door to door and church to church" among both blacks and whites in search of contributions. After eleven months of solicitations, he had collected enough money to buy twenty acres of land one mile east of Utica from a white woman for three hundred dollars.[21] His school opened in October 1903 with twenty local students, including a boy and a girl who boarded with Holtzclaw and his wife in a log cabin. Holtzclaw was thirty-three years old when he secured a charter for the Utica Normal and Industrial Institute, an "establishment of . . . learning . . . for the education of colored people."[22]

Although Holtzclaw never had a significant white patron like Edwards's chief benefactor, Randall O. Simpson, he did gain the support and trust of the local black clergy, "whose word was law to every colored man and woman in the community." He noted the importance of this sustenance: "If you cannot get on with the colored preachers in a place, your chances of success are slim in that community."[23] Holtzclaw escaped the nasty battle with the black clergy that Edwards could not avoid in Snow Hill when he had started his school.

As principal of Utica Institute, Holtzclaw seemed adept at tapping a variety of indigenous black supporters. Local blacks comprised thirteen of the school's fifteen original trustees, including Deacon A. C. Carter and Dan Lee, "the leading colored carpenter of the community."[24] These "unassuming, hardworking, honest individuals" conferred with Holtzclaw "without fail, rain or shine . . . in our effort to keep up the enthusiasm and thus . . . carry on the school." Subscription lists were printed and "every person kept one and placed thereon the name of any person who wished to become interested in the upbuilding of the school."[25] Holtzclaw frequently relied upon local blacks to support assorted fund-raising efforts on behalf of his fledgling institution.[26]

Holtzclaw believed that the building of his school could be accurately understood only in relation to certain geopolitical "conditions."[27] The setting for Utica Institute was on the boundary line between Hinds and Copiah counties in central Mississippi. Black people comprised an overwhelming majority of the population of these two counties in 1900 and 1910.[28] Utica was thirty miles southwest of Jackson, the state capitol. Although Holtzclaw frequently boasted that his school was situated "in the heart of the black belt of Mississippi, where the negroes outnumber the whites seven to one," he also realized that his predominantly black environment did not mean escape from the state's political and racial policies."[29]

The Mississippi Constitution of 1890 had disenfranchised black people, and a state law not only required segregated schools but also permitted local school boards to use their own discretion in the distribution of school funds. In 1910 school expenditures throughout the state averaged $10.60 for each white student and only $2.25 for each black student.[30] By 1910 the illiteracy rate for blacks in Hinds County had reached 31.7 percent; it was only 2.5 percent for whites.[31]

The founding of Utica Institute also coincided with the rise to power of James Kimble Vardaman, an anti-black newspaper editor-lawyer who served as governor of Mississippi from 1904 to 1908. Vardaman preached white supremacy and argued that money formerly spent to educate black people had been wasted because "no improvement could be noted in the moral nature of the Negro. . . . Then why squander money on his education when the only effect is to spoil a good field hand and make an insolent cook?"[32] Vardaman's anti-black stance symbolized the growing hostility toward blacks in Mississippi in the first decade of the twentieth century.[33]

How did Holtzclaw react to this acrimony, and what strategies did he pursue? The Utica principal diplomatically positioned himself among the virulent forces of his racially hostile environment. He invited a local banker to become the school treasurer and several prominent business owners to join his board of trustees. They accepted.[34] He successfully enlisted the support of such notable white Mississippians as Methodist Bishop Charles Galloway and Mayor R. W. Millsaps (the wealthy founder of Millsaps College) in fund-raising efforts.[35] He could not depend exclusively upon a planter aristocracy as Edwards did in Snow Hill. Rather, Holtzclaw envisioned himself as a black leader who could "understand and . . . get in touch with . . . white officials and press [his] cause."[36] At least one Tuskegee official, Emmett J. Scott — Washington's private secretary — applauded Holtzclaw's ability "in getting hold of the white people of that section."[37]

Race frequently intruded into Holtzclaw's transactions as an educator. Once he arranged to purchase land from a local white resident who reneged on the deal at the last moment. Holtzclaw considered suing, but his white attorney advised against such action, arguing that "it was better to lose the land and wait for other opportunities than to incur the ill-will of my white friends."[38] He lived in a social environment marked by fear. Utica Institute students were often afraid to move "to and fro among our white fellow-citizens in this section of the country." When Booker T. Washington visited the school in 1908, many local blacks opposed the visit because they thought that he would "never pass safely through the streets of Utica."[39]

Lynchings further heightened racial tensions. From 1899 to 1915, 209 blacks were reported lynched in Mississippi, including 4 in Hinds County.[40] Although Holtzclaw claimed in his autobiography (published in 1915) that he had appealed to the governor of Mississippi, E. F. Noel, "to check mob violence amongst us," he also contended that "there is not a state in the Union . . . that offers greater advantages to its Negro population than Mississippi."[41] When Holtzclaw designed a postcard (perhaps for fund-raising) dated January 1, 1912, with his picture and a brief accompanying text, it was not surprising that he felt the need to state that "any man that would do anything to, in any way, strain the relations between the two races in the South is an enemy to both races and an enemy to his country."[42] He never surrendered his belief that a black educator in rural Mississippi needed to "adjust . . . to the conditions that existed in the community."[43]

"The Force That Wins"

Holtzclaw started his school with twenty students in 1903. A year later he claimed an enrollment of 225, and a faculty member reported that 400 students enrolled in 1907. The average enrollment for the period 1903–15 was 363.[44] Female students comprised as much as 57 percent of the student body in 1914–15 and as little as 52 percent in 1908–9. Enrollment in the elementary grades (first through eighth) always exceeded that of the three-year teacher training program or the trade courses.

Utica Institute, like its counterpart at Snow Hill, was a boarding school. By 1910 more than half the student body resided on campus, but their needs were not easily met. For example, on one occasion the female students on campus came to their principal and told him that "they would have to give up the effort to get an education. It was very cold, there was not enough fuel to go around, and not enough bedding." Holtzclaw calmed this discontent by buying fifty quilts that were then "laid over the sleeping girls in twenty-five beds."[45]

Holtzclaw believed that his students needed a disciplined routine that taught reliability and regularity. He devised, therefore, a "habit-forming routine" for his residential students that included a rigorous daily schedule:

The rising bell rings 5:10 A.M.; 5:50, the first breakfast bell; 6, the breakfast bell; twenty-five minutes for breakfast; 6:25 to 6:45, preparation for daily inspection of rooms; 6:50, work bell rings; 7:25, morning study hour; 8:20, school bell rings; 8:25, young men inspected on battalion grounds as to their toilet; 8:40, morning devotion; 8:55, current news period; 9:20, classroom work begins; 12, all work closes; 12:10, dinner; 1:00 P.M., work bell rings; 1:30, class work begins; 3:30, class work ends; 5:30, bell rings to stop work; 6, supper; 6:30, study hour; 7, night school begins (for those who work in the day and go to school at night); 8:40, evening devotion; 9:20, first retiring bell; 9:30, retiring bell.[46]

Holtzclaw was convinced that such a routine would actually transform the basic nature of his students. Life at Utica Institute, he believed, could completely regenerate its student body: "I like to watch a girl, who enters school so crude as to seem almost deformed, pass from one stage to another from year to year, until after a while she stands forth on Commencement day literally transformed in soul and body—a new creature, because of the new atmosphere in which she has been permitted to live." Holtzclaw made character building a prominent part of his edu-

cational program, because "we see the mass of darkest ignorance surrounding us." Education, he stated, could "actually
make better and more efficient men and women of . . .
Negroes."[47]

However, few students actually graduated. Holtzclaw reported that by 1910 his school had only twenty-eight graduates,
whereas four hundred "other young people . . . have received
more or less industrial training." Utica still had only forty-six
graduates by 1914, twenty of whom resided in Mississippi.[48] He
explained that his students found it difficult to stay in school
because of their skills: "The demand for good workmen is so
great that they are tempted to leave as soon as they become
reasonably proficient."[49]

Although few in number, Utica Institute graduates testified
that they carried the "spirit that makes service the foundation
upon which all usefulness should rest."[50] Two normal school
graduates started their own schools in Mississippi. Another
wrote that "I have my hands full, but I am doing well, I think,
trying to teach one hundred and forty young people, daily; but I
enjoy being a servant of the people of this community."[51] Holtzclaw also reported that a "majority" of his graduates "[did] not
hesitate to go into the forsaken spots . . . away back into the
rural districts and there render unselfish service."[52]

Although one former Utica student informed Holtzclaw
that she was "so glad I attended school at Utica and learned how
to do something," he readily admitted to one of his trustees that
the majority of the trade courses were of the "infant industry"
variety and were often taught in a "most haphazard way." He
added: "Sometimes a teacher had to be placed in charge of some
division about which he or she knew almost nothing, and had to
gain sufficient experience day by day to teach the pupils."[53] Visitors from the U.S. Bureau of Education in 1915 also noted that
"sufficient emphasis has not been given to the educational side"
of industrial training.[54]

Trade courses at Utica were not initiated until 1906, because
the school owned "no apparatus, nor shops, nor money." Holtzclaw traveled north seeking assistance and encountered a white
minister in New York City who befriended him. This cleric and
his congregation "felt it would be desirable for the students to

learn the printer's trade [and] gave us a little press and two or three cases of type." One parishioner also donated "some apparatus to start a sewing room."[55] Holtzclaw recognized without complaint that white financial support sometimes dictated the curricular offerings of black industrial schools, and he understood the relationship between his efforts and the approbation of white people: "Whenever education, educators, and educational processes can produce something that white men want, they favor the education of the Negro."[56]

Holtzclaw seemed less interested in developing the academic aspects of his school than Edwards was at Snow Hill. There was no public declaration, for example, that industrial education was not meant to confine the ambitions of black people. Utica was "not a college, but a simple Normal and Industrial Institute," where male students studied, among other subjects, carpentry, blacksmithing, and wheelwrighting; where female students took courses in sewing, millinery, and cooking; and where all were exposed to "knowledge of how to teach the common school branches."[57]

Holtzclaw was the only teacher for his initial class of twenty in the fall of 1903. He claimed to have an all-black staff of seven—including himself and his wife—for a student population of 225 in 1904, eleven teachers for 400 students a year later, and a faculty member referred to a staff of twenty-five "teachers and officers" in 1907.[58]

Female members of Holtzclaw's staff held a number of important positions between 1903 and 1915. A visitor to Utica Institute in May 1905 commented that "the lady principal of the institute, Miss Ada L. Hicks, was one of the most helpful workers associated with the professor [Holtzclaw]. She is deeply concerned about the work and is painstaking in every effort." The visitor also noted that "Miss Clara J. Lee was head of the academic work of the institute. . . . Her services have been invaluable and her endeavors are highly appreciated by the principal." Eight of the thirteen faculty members in the Academic Department in 1909 were women, and Holtzclaw reported to Tuskegee Institute in 1910 that his wife was "Director of The Girls' Industries" and that Effie H. Davis [his sister] was the "principal of the night school."[59]

Holtzclaw used his alma mater as a major source for his

faculty between 1903 and 1915. Four of the seven teachers who comprised the Utica staff in 1904–5 were graduates of Tuskegee Institute. One of these faculty members reported in January 1905 to George Washington Carver—her former teacher—that "Tuskegee is well represented here—there are four of us. So I imagine we are a Smaller Tuskegee."[60] Five of the thirteen teachers in the Academic Department in 1909 were Tuskegee graduates, including Emma C. Penney, a classmate of Holtzclaw's and the daughter of Edgar Penney, the director of the Phelps Bible Training School at Tuskegee. Holtzclaw also reported that he often left his "most trusted lieutenant," D. W. L. Davis, superintendent of industries and a Tuskegee Institute graduate, in charge of the campus whenever he left on fund-raising ventures.[61]

But many members of the Utica Institute faculty came from schools other than Tuskegee. The "lady principal" of Utica in 1905, Ada L. Hicks, graduated from Snow Hill Institute, and Clara J. Lee, the head of the Academic Department in that year, completed a teaching course at Tougaloo University in Mississippi. As of March 1909, the Academic Department had faculty from historically black institutions such as Fisk University, Mary Holmes College, Wilberforce University, and Alcorn State College. There was also one graduate from the predominantly white University of Iowa.[62]

A visitor to Utica Institute in 1912 commented on the youth of the faculty: "This is the work of young negroes. These teachers are practically boys and girls themselves, recent graduates of Tuskegee, of American Missionary Association schools, and of various smaller schools. . . ." This visitor also sensed a special relationship between black students and their black teachers: "A conviction has taken me, after much observation at Utica, that negro students under negro teachers seem in all their performances to display an exhilarating freedom of body and soul."[63]

Holtzclaw revealed something about the economic straits of several of his faculty members. While he was away from Utica on a fund-raising tour in the early history of the school, he received a letter from one of his teachers. "Dear Principal," it read, "I regret to have to bother you, but I am actually barefooted and cannot go from one building to another. If you can send me enough money to get a pair of shoes, I will not bother you again soon." Holtzclaw admitted that the salary of the school's blacksmith was originally "so small that when he was called to neighboring towns on Saturdays to do horseshoeing, he used to bring back, as a result of his work, more than half the amount of his monthly wages."[64] There is evidence that the economic hardships of the Utica staff may not have been limited to the early days of the school. Half the school's indebtedness in 1915 was the result of salaries owed to teachers.[65]

In spite of a less than adequate instructional program, an inability to pay his teachers, and infrequent graduates, Holtzclaw initiated four ventures intended to "help the people in general to rise": the Teachers' Extension Movement, the Utica Negro Farmers' Conferences, the Black Belt Improvement Society, and the Community Court of Justice.

The Teachers' Extension Movement was formed by dividing the area surrounding Utica Institute into sections. A faculty member was assigned to each section and held responsible for its advancement "morally and otherwise." Teachers were "to do all within their powers to show the people in that locality how to better their condition." Working with a local minister, they were to become "a sort of moral leader of the people." Holtzclaw claimed that the amount of work his teachers did was "something astonishing. They labored . . . incessantly, in season and out of season."[66]

Holtzclaw also organized an annual Negro Farmers' Conference, as did both Washington and Edwards. The principal of Utica Institute, the son of a sharecropper, called together local farmers in 1905 and initiated the first Utica Negro Farmers' Conference. Holtzclaw was elected president, and subsequent farmers' conferences featured speeches and testimonies by farmers who had bought farms or built houses the preceding year. Holtzclaw used these farmers' conferences as a forum to encourage blacks to stay in Mississippi. At the annual Farmers' Conference in 1909, for example, Holtzclaw was quoted by the *Jackson Daily News* as saying, "There is plenty of land for sale all over the state of Mississippi at reasonable prices. Here is a great opportunity for us to plant ourselves firmly in the soil."[67]

The Utica Negro Farmers' Conferences were held not only to hear speeches and stories but also to help black farmers become more proficient at raising food and caring for their livestock. Holtzclaw invited black professionals to address the farmers' conferences. In 1908, for example, a black physician from Vicksburg, Mississippi, addressed the conference on the prevention and cure of hookworm; a black druggist from the same city suggested cures for diseased horses; and George Washington Carver, head of the Department of Agricultural Research at Tuskegee Institute, "spent two hours before the assembled farmers, with a sweet potato in his hand, about which he delivered a most effective lecture."[68]

Holtzclaw organized the Black Belt Improvement Society as an adjunct to the Negro Farmers' Conference. The name and purpose of this organization duplicated an organization that had existed at Snow Hill Institute. Holtzclaw had had an opportunity to observe firsthand how a community-based organization could function when he worked at Snow Hill from 1898 to 1902. He initiated his Improvement Society to encourage economic self-sufficiency among rural blacks by selling land to black farmers.[69]

Perhaps the most unique example of the extension activities sponsored by Utica Institute was the Community Court of Justice. This "court" handled misdemeanors for blacks who lived near the school, because the school was situated "five miles from the town and had no magistrate within easy reach." Cases were brought, testimonies taken, and decisions rendered before this tribunal. Holtzclaw was selected as the "judge," "lawyers" were appointed for defendants and plaintiffs, and testimony was heard by a "jury" of five persons. When the "jury" failed to deliver a verdict on an alleged wife-beating charge, Holtzclaw decided in favor of the wife and "ordered the man to stand still and let his wife strike him thirty-nine times. This she proceeded to do and court adjourned, and no case of wife-beating has come under my notice since." Holtzclaw was convinced that the Community Court of Justice "taught valuable lessons and created a spirit of general progress in the right direction."[70]

At least one historian has maintained that the Community Court also illustrated Holtzclaw's "refusal to take black disputes to whites for resolution or to allow planters to punish blacks for petty crimes."[71] It is doubtful that Holtzclaw would have ever publicly admitted such an intention. Each of his extension activities was based on the assumption, held by many black industrial educators in the South, that "community service and uplift, joined with . . . black self-help, yielded large returns." He avidly adopted a community service approach: "Our school aims to be the center of influence in a neglected area."[72]

Holtzclaw became an impresario of educational outreach, a function that may have been his most impressive achievement. He desperately wanted black people to be self-sufficient, to "depend upon themselves, [and] to find in their own communities and about their own doors a means of progress and betterment, and not to look to any outside source whatever."[73] However, within the confines of his school, he was not always able to translate his ideas into practice. His school had few graduates, and a lack of finances often dictated its curriculum. He labored, as well, in a vineyard of racial hostility, which prompted him to accommodate rather than to challenge.

The genesis of Utica Institute differed from that of Snow Hill, another Tuskegee by-product. Edwards returned to his home immediately after graduation from Tuskegee and started his school in a familiar setting at the age of twenty-four. Holtzclaw was thirty-three years old when he founded his school in 1903. Perhaps his three years of teaching in Georgia and his four years of work at Snow Hill Institute enabled him to endure the frustrations that he encountered upon finding a community conducive to his work. When he finally settled in Utica, however, he proved adept at winning local black support without alienating influential whites. He believed that in order to maintain a school community "there must be a leader . . . who has the confidence of all factions" and who is willing "to stay on the firing line and fight the good fight of faith."[74]

UTICA INSTITUTE AFTER 1915: William Holtzclaw died in 1943, after serving forty years as principal. Three years later Utica became the Hinds County Agricultural School, a public institution. In 1958 the school was again reorganized and became Utica Junior College. The college is now officially known as the Utica Campus of the Hinds Junior College District.

Chapter Three

The Tuskegee
Machine in Action

THE EDUCATIONAL POLICIES AND PRAC-
tices adopted by Edwards and Holtzclaw were significantly influenced by the relationship between the two men and Booker T.
Washington. Tuskegee graduates were the "pride and concern"
of its founder. As Tuskegee's monthly publication, the *Southern
Letter,* stated in 1893, "Each student . . . reproduces Tuskegee,
in some sense, in some dark place." Edwards and Holtzclaw
were the subjects of considerable scrutiny as they struggled to
create paradigms of their alma mater.[1]

Inquiry into Washington's influence over the affairs of
Snow Hill and Utica provides a perspective on the machinations
of what historian Louis Harlan has called "The Tuskegee Machine," an "intricate, nation-wide web of institutions in the
black community that were conducted, dominated, or strongly
influenced from the little town in the deep South where Washington had his base."[2] Washington's most perceptive biographer
claims that the features of the Tuskegee Machine included its
stringent control of black political patronage, Washington's influence over the black press, and various secret activities. The
machine made "rewards and punishments a central feature of its
recruitment and retention of its followers."[3] Synonymous with
power and intrigue, the Tuskegee Machine also operated in the
educational arena. The ties between Washington and Edwards
and Holtzclaw, then, merit scrutiny as a case study of Tuskegee's
influence on important educational outposts.

One of the methods that Washington used to call attention
to the work of his graduates was to publicize their efforts in his

books, in school publications, and in his articles for nationally circulated periodicals. In *Working with the Hands* (1904), sub-titled a "sequel to *Up From Slavery*," Washington sketched the work of nine Tuskegee graduates, including Edwards and Holtz-claw, in a chapter entitled "Spreading the Tuskegee Spirit." He included pictures of the Snow Hill campus, provided facts about finances, and noted that Snow Hill had "the support and sym-pathy" of "all the best white people in the county." Washington mentioned Utica Institute as well, quoting Holtzclaw's descrip-tion of the founding of his school.[4]

Significant publicity for Tuskegee offshoots appeared the next year in *Tuskegee and Its People* (1905). The main portion of this book consisted of seventeen autobiographical accounts of graduates, five of whom founded schools modeled after Tuskegee. Edwards contributed a chapter entitled "Uplifting the Submerged Masses." Holtzclaw called his contribution "A School Principal's Story." Washington unabashedly celebrated the achievement of these school founders, calling their accounts "vivid pen-portraits of the young men . . . who have gone out of Tuskegee carrying into diversified lives the principles and pre-cepts imbibed from their parent school." Their work illustrated the "wholesome and evangelizing influence of Tuskegee's preachments."[5]

Another effort to promote the work of Tuskegee graduates came with the publication in 1911 of Monroe Nathan Work's *Industrial Work of Tuskegee Graduates and Former Students during the Year 1910*. Work, a graduate of the University of Chicago and the head of Tuskegee's Division of Research and Records, was hired specifically "to study the effects of the school's programs through the work and achievements of its graduates." One chapter featured graduates who had founded schools. The efforts of Edwards and Holtzclaw merited exten-sive treatment, including information about enrollment, courses of study, and extension activities.[6]

Washington occasionally wrote articles in widely circulated periodicals featuring the work of his prized former students. In January 1900, "Signs of Progress Among the Negroes" appeared in *Century Magazine*. Washington recalled how Edwards had appeared at Tuskegee "with his blistered feet and small white bundle, which contained all the clothing he possessed," and how he had started Snow Hill Institute "in a vacant log cabin." According to Washington, Snow Hill represented a "foundation for the solution of the legal and political difficulties that exist in the South" and exemplified "what has already been accomplished in the South under the most difficult circumstances."[7] Edwards clearly emerged a hero.

In "A Cheerful Journey Through Mississippi" (1909), Washington detailed for *World's Work* his impressions (from a seven-day visit in 1908) of black people's progress in the state. Washington had visited the Utica principal, and he wrote a brief but laudatory account of Holtzclaw's journey from Tuskegee to Mississippi to establish a school "that could be conducted along the lines of Tuskegee Institute." He added: "From the very first, he succeeded in gaining the sympathy of both races for the work that he was trying to do. . . . In addition to this, he has already started an endowment-fund in order to make the work that he is doing there permanent, and to give aid by means of scholarships to worthy students who are not fully able to pay their own way."[8]

Washington's public pronouncements about Edwards and Holtzclaw and their schools served several purposes. Such publicity sought to prove "the worth of the Tuskegee educational program as well as to justify the public's continued financial support of Washington's educational community." As founders of miniature Tuskegees, Edwards and Holtzclaw were held in high esteem. The stories of their struggles, sacrifices, and hard work exemplified the success of a Tuskegee education.[9] Washington's affirmation also bound the two principals to their mentor. They gained the type of public attention that it would have been difficult to obtain on their own.

In his relations with Edwards and Holtzclaw, Washington played a variety of roles besides that of publicist: he was also fund-raiser, advisor, and critic. He exercised additional influence by sending key staff members and inspection committees to their schools, and he used the Tuskegee Machine to discourage their participation in an association of black industrial schools.

In the summer of 1897 Edwards made his first "Northern

Campaign" when he traveled with a Tuskegee group to New England to raise money. This trip allowed him to meet several philanthropists, especially in Boston. He made at least one trip by himself each year thereafter until he resigned from his position because of ill health in 1924.[10]

Edwards relied upon Washington's actual presence to help his school raise money. In November 1899, for example, he asked his mentor to appear with him at church in Boston because a white clergyman assured him that the visit would be a success only if Washington consented to speak. Edwards was so anxious for Washington to accompany him that he agreed to share any proceeds with Tuskegee. He stated his dependency bluntly: "I need not tell you because you know what it would mean to my school to be put before the public in this way." A week later Edwards still had received no response from Washington, and he grew uneasy. He wrote to Washington: "This proposed meeting is the hope of my success on this trip and if I fail in this I fear that I will return to Snow Hill without success. I find it hard to get to the people. If you will just have a few words to say that will suffice."[11] Washington did not appear with Edwards in Boston on that occasion, and evidently such entreaties stopped for a time. Edwards wrote to Washington in 1902 that two years had passed since he had asked his mentor to speak for Snow Hill, and he again requested an appearance: "I sincerely trust that you may be able to be with me on that day and that you will allow me to advertise it in that way. I beg that you give that much of your time to Snow Hill."[12]

If Washington was not always available or willing to accompany Edwards on fund-raising programs, he did act at times as an intermediary for philanthropic donations. While soliciting aid from Andrew Carnegie, the wealthy industrialist, Edwards believed that a strong letter from Washington to Carnegie about Snow Hill would have "a decisive result." It did. Carnegie donated ten thousand dollars in 1906. Washington further encouraged the industrialist's interest a year later when he suggested that Edwards was someone who had "achieved great success."[13]

Acting as a broker of funds for Snow Hill, Washington wrote to Jacob Henry Schiff, a major contributor to Tuskegee and the founder of the Southern Education Fund, suggesting that one hundred dollars be sent to Snow Hill annually because the school was "sending out good men and women as teachers and industrial workers." Edwards informed Washington that he had been receiving this annual gift and that Schiff had sent him an additional five hundred dollars in 1915. Washington also helped Edwards receive money from the Rosenwald and Slater funds.[14]

Despite Washington's assistance, Snow Hill always experienced serious financial difficulties, especially after a fire devastated the campus in 1911. Edwards described the damage in a telegram: "Snow Hill school for Negroes lost by fire last night. Dining Hall and Commissary Buildings, Library and food supplies were in these buildings and entirely lost. Value of property destroyed, $10,000. Insurance $2,000. Dr. Washington, please put this on the Associated Press wire." Washington expressed his sympathy and informed Edwards that he was seeking assistance for Snow Hill.[15]

Holtzclaw was no less dependent upon Washington for assistance in raising money. In 1904, a year after he had founded his school, Holtzclaw was permitted to address audiences sympathetic to Tuskegee in northern cities like Boston and Philadelphia. He readily made known his affiliation when he wrote an appeal for funds in 1908: "I am a graduate of Tuskegee Institute, Alabama; and I am doing similar work here, my work being the only outgrowth of Tuskegee in this section of the country." He asked Washington to sign this appeal because, as he argued, "I am sure it will do untold good for our work." Washington agreed to do so.[16] Holtzclaw again sought Washington's support in writing a year later when he requested a "formal letter of endorsement based on your personal knowledge of my work." The Tuskegee principal responded with a "To Whom it May Concern" letter that stated: "I cannot speak too cordially of the effective way in which Mr. Holtzclaw and his co-workers are attacking the problems presented to them. The school is located in a section where it has an opportunity to do effective work among the Negro people. Mr. Holtzclaw is deserving of encouragement and support."[17]

Washington also influenced some of the same philanthropists who helped Edwards to assist Utica Institute. He recommended that Schiff's Southern Education Fund send one hundred dollars annually to Utica: "I visited [this institution] a year ago and found it doing good work. It was started by William H. Holtzclaw, one of our graduates." Washington informed another donor that "I think it wise for you to continue to help Holtzclaw. He is doing good work."[18]

When natural disaster struck the Utica campus, as happened at Snow Hill, Washington offered assistance. Holtzclaw informed Washington on June 10, 1910, that "a cyclone struck us last night and completely destroyed two buildings and damaged a third." Washington's response was businesslike: "I am sorry to learn that a cyclone has visited you and destroyed two of your buildings. . . . These visitations are quite disastrous, but I hope you may soon have under way plans for the restoration of the damage done." A month later Washington contacted Schiff and requested an extra fifty dollars for Holtzclaw because "they have recently had a storm that blew down several of their buildings."[19] When Holtzclaw went to Boston in August 1910, in search of funds for his damaged campus, he discovered that Washington was in Huntington, Long Island, and promptly requested that Washington contact the Boston Chamber of Commerce, an organization that was "considering the advisability of making a substantial contribution to our work on account of the cyclone." Although there is no evidence that Washington wrote to the Boston Chamber, he responded by noting that "you abundantly deserve whatever encouragement you may be able to receive at their hands" and also suggested another potential source of funding in Boston.[20]

Holtzclaw's need for financial support continued throughout his association with his mentor. As late as 1915, Holtzclaw appealed to Washington for renewed assistance: "We are running far behind this year in current expenses and teacher's [sic] salaries. In fact, much farther behind than ever before. . . . If you can prevail with the General Education Board to help us out, I shall be very grateful indeed."[21]

Washington's role as an intermediary for funds to Snow Hill and Utica reflected his influence as "the sole arbiter on questions of donations to Tuskegee's off-shoots. Many philanthropic contributions . . . were channelled through his office."[22] The Tuskegee founder, in effect, made his role as fund-raiser a significant element of his Tuskegee Machine, and the financial straits of his protégés made them dependent on his network of power and prestige.

Washington also acted as an advisor and critic on school management. He wrote to Edwards "in the most friendly spirit" in May 1908, suggesting that he be "very careful to see that everything about the School is absolutely clean, and everything is carefully systematized inside and outside." Edwards replied that he would do all in his power to "improve the conditions" of his school.[23] When one of Snow Hill's normal school graduates decided to expand a school that he had founded in a community not far from Snow Hill, Washington cautioned Edwards, "I think it would be a mistake to encourage the building of a school so close to yours."[24] When financial difficulties plagued Snow Hill in 1915, Washington advised his former student in February to secure a loan, in June to sell "a portion of your land," and in October to "let nothing swerve you from your purpose to cut down expenses."[25]

Washington seemed particularly interested in having Edwards assemble a strong board of trustees. This was a constant problem for Edwards, in sharp contrast to the success that his mentor had in attracting influential persons to his own board.[26] The Tuskegee principal suggested a "strong business Board, not sentimental people, but people who have heart combined with head." Edwards admitted that "I have not succeeded as rapidly in this direction as I had hoped for."[27] When he failed to hold a meeting of his trustees as planned in June 1910, Washington chastised him: "It will be impossible for you to get men of any quality and reputation to serve on your board unless you hold regular meetings." He also disapproved of listing "Trustees" and "References" together on the Snow Hill letterhead: "You ought to make some distinction between trustees and people who are merely put down to be referred to. . . . 'Trustees and References' is not good grammar."[28] Edwards soon assured Washington that he would be more definite about setting a time for meetings of his board of trustees and called attention to his new letterhead that separated "Trustees" from "References," a rearrangement that "I trust . . . is pleasing to you." But it was often difficult for Edwards to satisfy Washington. When he selected three clergymen as trustees, Washington responded that "I do not believe it of much value to get too many preachers on the board."[29]

Washington criticized Holtzclaw far less severely. To be sure, Holtzclaw did not always please the Tuskegee principal, who questioned him about his school's unbalanced budget in 1908. Holtzclaw felt compelled to explain his indebtedness and trusted "that this explanation will be satisfactory." The financial condition of Utica again attracted Washington's attention seven years later when he wrote curtly to Holtzclaw: "I make note that you are running behind in current expenses and teachers' salaries."[30] Washington might have also criticized Holtzclaw's board of trustees, because Holtzclaw wrote him that "With reference to the letter of the 21st, you will be glad to know that . . . we eliminated from the Board the name of every useless Trustee. I feel that as a Board, we are now thoroughly organized. . . . I shall do as you advise, that is, try to have two Trustee meetings a year."[31]

Washington might have been more lenient toward Holtzclaw than toward Edwards because of the special relationship that had developed between the Utica principal and Emmett J. Scott, Washington's personal secretary—a connection that was significant because of Scott's status. A native of Houston, Texas, Scott had once edited a black newspaper in his hometown, where he had so successfully managed the publicity for a visit by Washington that the Tuskegee principal hired him. According to Louis Harlan, Scott became Washington's "closest private advisor" and assisted him "in all matters of racial strategy." In effect, Scott served as "the general manager of the Tuskegee Machine."[32]

In April 1912, Scott praised Utica as a satisfactory paradigm of Tuskegee Institute in a letter to Julius Rosenwald, the president of Sears, Roebuck and Co.: "The school is being carried on along sane and practical lines. Cleanliness, order and system are to be found everywhere and Mr. Holtzclaw [is] . . . striving hard to emphasize those ideals that we at Tuskegee emphasize. . . . All in all, I must say that I regard Utica as one of the very strongest of the Tuskegee off-shoots." When Holtzclaw received Scott's letter, he responded, "I am sure that such a letter will do a great deal of good."[33] The Utica principal did not have to wait very long before he learned of the effect of Scott's commendation. Rosenwald informed Holtzclaw that to "indicate my interest in your work, I shall be glad to contribute $1,000 annually for five years." Holtzclaw recognized his debt to Scott: "To secure an endorsement of one thousand dollars for five years is no small item. I want to express to you my gratitude and that of both teachers and students."[34] Scott also appealed to the Slater Fund and the Phelps Stokes Fund for assistance in meeting expenses during the financially troubled years of 1914 and 1915.[35]

The ties that bound Edwards and Holtzclaw to Tuskegee extended beyond the multiple roles of its founder. To assist his former student, Washington dispatched several key staff members to the Snow Hill campus on at least five occasions between 1909 and 1915. Edwards gratefully acknowledged the assistance of Robert Bedford, a white minister and Tuskegee trustee, sent to assist with a large land purchase in January 1909.[36] When Edwards needed a surveying team to mark the boundaries of his campus in 1912, Washington dispatched several of his own workers. He also asked his school's treasurer and Scott to attend a Snow Hill board of trustees meeting in 1912 that he could not attend.[37] Edwards accepted the services of Tuskegee's auditor, who looked into the accounting system in 1913, and he eagerly anticipated the visit of Washington's brother, John B. Washington (Superintendent of Industries at Tuskegee) who had a "little money given by a special fund to bring about some improvements."[38] Each of these visits elicited effusive praise from the Snow Hill principal.

Tuskegee personnel visited Holtzclaw's school less frequently. He attributed George Washington Carver's appearance at the Utica Negro Farmers' Conference of 1913 to Washington: "I am writing this letter to especially thank you for permitting Professor Carver to come, and I wish that I could explain to you something of the good that he did by his visit." Washington welcomed the news. Holtzclaw also appreciated the annual visits of Bedford, who served as chairman of his board of trustees.[39]

Not all visits by Tuskegee personnel proved gratifying for Edwards, however. Three Tuskegee staff members who visited Snow Hill in 1910 criticized the academic program for being too theoretical.[40] This inspection committee discovered an even more serious apostasy from the Tuskegee tradition: Snow Hill offered two-year courses in Latin and German "for those planning to take up higher work in the professions." The visitors objected strongly to such a deviation from Washington's educational approach: "From what we observed we do not think that the average student there [Snow Hill] is ready for these subjects nor do we think that the school is thoroughly ready to teach them. Our opinion is that the school should . . . try to perfect the students as far as possible upon the fundamental lines and not branch off on these higher subjects."[41]

Three weeks after the visit, Edwards wrote to his mentor and explained his errancy in allowing Latin and German into the curriculum. These languages "came in incidentally" because Edwards had to find a teaching assignment for a new staff member. "They were not, strictly speaking, in the course of study," he wrote. "These languages have never been catalogued and it never was my intention of placing them in the catalogue. . . . I do not put any stress upon the languages and I never have done so."[42]

Fearing estrangement from Washington, Edwards stated that the teaching of Latin and German was not a stratagem to gain autonomy from the Tuskegee brand of education but rather an intrusion into a vocationally oriented course of study: "I think that the Committee must have gotten the impression that I was attempting to push these languages to the front, and such has never been the case. . . . I hope I haven't and will not, make the impression that I am in any way trying to make these languages conspicuous in our work." Edwards dispensed with the languages immediately, regretted that the incident had caused Washington to mistrust his judgment, and expressed the hope that "the same will not occur again in the future."[43]

It is interesting to note, however, that the enrollment of normal school students at Snow Hill reached its highest point after 1908. Perhaps the introduction of Latin and German was more than an accident, since Edwards knew that a normal school student might be attracted to studying languages. In addition, as Joseph Citro has discovered, Tuskegee had become more of an industrial school and less of a normal school after 1903. The report of the Tuskegee visitors might have reflected this trend.[44]

Tuskegee officials continued their criticism of Edwards and his school. In 1912 the Snow Hill principal acknowledged that recent visitors disliked the slovenly appearance of his campus, but he assured Washington that the school had devoted much time to general cleaning and also to repairing broken glass and windows.[45]

Relations between Edwards and Washington were strained almost to the breaking point after Robert E. Park, a white confidant and ghostwriter for Washington, censured Snow Hill's operation in a report to Tuskegee in 1913. Edwards wrote to his mentor that he was shocked to learn from Park "that you are considering withdrawing your support from Snow Hill." Although Edwards admitted that the school had many shortcomings, he added that it was "striving as never before to correct them." Edwards defended his administration, saying that he had worked hard to make the school one of which Washington and Tuskegee could be proud. However, he concluded, if Washington intended to withdraw support, Edwards would resign immediately, because the school was needed in that region and it required all the support that Washington could give to it.[46]

Washington's response eight days later reflected his insistence that Snow Hill Institute present the appearance of an efficient and orderly school:

Everyone who goes to Snow Hill is disappointed in these respects:
1 — The grounds are not kept clean and attractive.
2 — The repairs are not kept up — windows are out and houses are unpainted.
3 — You do not give enough attention to the growing of ordinary farm and garden crops.
4 — Another thing that would help the appearance of conditions at Snow Hill is to see that everything is finished up. There are too many unfinished jobs there now — it is much wiser to finish up one thing no matter how small it is before undertaking something else.[47]

But Washington had spent time and energy publicizing the work at Snow Hill, assisting in fund-raising efforts, and evaluating school operations, and he did not want to sever his ties with Edwards. He concluded his letter benignly: "We are all proud of Snow Hill and we are gratified at its success in the past, but want to see it do better. I always speak a good word for Snow Hill wherever and whenever I can, but I wish to be sure that my recommendations are based upon the truth."[48]

Relations between Edwards and Holtzclaw and Tuskegee involved more than the internal operation of their schools. Their affiliation with Tuskegee also affected their dealings with the Association of Negro Industrial and Secondary Schools. The purpose of this organization was "to promote self-help in . . . Negro schools, to increase their efficiency, and to bring about in their behalf a wider public interest and support."[49] ANISS developed out of the concern of certain white philanthropists for the worsening financial condition of black southern industrial schools by 1913. As Henry S. Enck describes the situation: "Northern donors were weary of the seemingly endless black appeals and were turning to other causes. Also, the ever-increasing demands of the schools frustrated a number of their northern friends." Philanthropist George Foster Peabody and Clarence H. Kelsey, a New York banker and longtime champion of black industrial education, advocated a consolidation of black fund-raising efforts as a way to help industrial schools such as Snow Hill and Utica remain financially viable.[50]

The leadership of ANISS was composed of black and white supporters of the NAACP, many of whom were anti–Booker T. Washington. On April 17, 1913, ANISS held its first meeting at the NAACP headquarters in New York City. Oscar Garrison Villard, a white founder of the NAACP and the grandson of the noted abolitionist William Lloyd Garrison, invited Washington to attend the organizational meeting. Washington refused to attend because he considered ANISS "an effort to undermine his influence in industrial education. . . . He considered it a mistake to identify educational problems of the South with the work of the Association (NAACP) and inferred that Villard was encroaching on Tuskegee's domain."[51]

It was time for the Tuskegee Machine to spring into action.

Edwards attended the initial meeting of ANISS along with thirty-nine other black industrial educators. Washington knew of Edwards's involvement, and in May 1915 he informed his Snow Hill protégé that he had obtained a copy of a letterhead of the association with Edwards's name listed as a member of the executive committee. "I confess I am somewhat puzzled," Washington concluded.[52] A penitent Edwards responded that he had not attended a meeting in two years and "had written Mr. Burnet [an ANISS member] but one letter in my life and that was today asking to have my name taken of [sic] his committee or rather letter head, as I was unable to serve. I trust that this will be done at once."[53] The fact that it took Edwards two years to resign officially from ANISS suggests that perhaps he believed that some sort of association with that group would reverse the faltering financial condition of his school. But to no avail. Washington continued campaigning against ANISS, and Edwards terminated his relationship with it.

Holtzclaw followed a different course altogether. Emmett Scott wrote to Holtzclaw on February 26, 1913, to inform him that "I have just learned that you are planning to attend a certain meeting at 20 Vesey Street [the headquarters of the NAACP], New York City, sometime soon." He then expressed his desire that "those persons who are allied with us and whom we are earnestly supporting in every way within our power not ally themselves with this movement. The purpose underlying and at the bottom of the whole thing is all apparent. . . . I am sure you can easily decide a method of relieving yourself of any obligation to be present at the meeting." Scott was so concerned about this matter that he hoped that "this letter will not pass out of your individual hands," and he even requested that Holtzclaw "reply in your own hand writing with the return of this letter."[54]

Holtzclaw wrote to Scott five days later, informing him that "With reference to the within note, I am under no obligation to attend the meeting and shall not do so. I thank you for calling it to my attention." Scott then informed Washington several days later that he had "kept Holtzclaw away."[55] Although Holtzclaw did not attend the April meeting in New York City, he was elected president of the ANISS executive committee in his absence. He advised Scott of this development: "I have just been

46

notified of my election and I am writing to ask your advise [*sic*] before accepting or declining. I do not want to get mixed up in something that will not be best for this Institution and for what I will designate the general Tuskegee interests in the South."[56] Washington himself responded a week later: "I advise that you let up the whole matter for a few weeks until you can see either Mr. Scott or myself. There will be plenty of time."[57]

When Holtzclaw did not hear from Tuskegee for three weeks, he wrote to Scott on May 25, 1913, with the news that the executive committee of ANISS had scheduled a meeting in Atlanta. Holtzclaw eagerly offered himself as an operative of the Tuskegee Machine: "I have thought that I might learn something by attending this meeting. . . . I . . . shall be very glad to run down to Tuskegee and have a talk with you about this organization."[58] While extant correspondence on this matter is scanty, Scott did make the notation "all right" on Holtzclaw's letter. Evidently, "general Tuskegee interests" dictated that Holtzclaw affiliate with ANISS, since the Utica principal supplied Scott with information about various facets of the organization on at least three different occasions between November 1913 and March 1914.

When Leslie Pinckney Hill, the secretary of ANISS and a black opponent of Washington, wrote a newspaper article linking the association with the NAACP, Holtzclaw reported to Scott in November 1913 that several black industrial school educators in ANISS had reprimanded Hill: "Several members expressed their opinion then and there to the effect that it would be a positive injury to all of us if it [newspaper article] should go out in that shape and so the matter was clearly impressed upon Mr. Hill that this must not obtain in the future. The matter was dropped there." The Utica principal pledged to Scott that "I will have considerable to say to you, whenever I can get a chance to see you about this whole affair."[59]

Scott replied to Holtzclaw early in December 1913 with a letter marked "Personal," in which he stated that "the difficulty will continue as long as meetings are held at the particular building of that organization" [the NAACP]. He closed with the hope that "I may have the opportunity of seeing you sometime soon that we may go over in person some of the matters mentioned by you."[60] Holtzclaw supplied additional information three days later. He informed Scott that some members of ANISS disliked meeting at the NAACP headquarters and that "I have noticed that there is a sentiment in the Association [ANISS] against anything that pertains to Vesey Street, but there seems to be one man, the Secretary [Leslie P. Hill], who is thoroughly in sympathy with everything down on that street."[61]

Holtzclaw, a loyal lieutenant in the Tuskegee Machine, seemed far from reluctant to abandon his reportorial role in his last extant letter to Scott (March 1914) regarding ANISS: "I am very anxious indeed to see you. I want to talk over the matter of these New York meetings we have been having."[62] A study of the available evidence suggests that Holtzclaw stayed firmly within the orbit of the Tuskegee Machine, even while he served on the executive committee of an organization that maintained an identity with the NAACP and opponents of Washington. Holtzclaw eventually resigned from ANISS in 1915, no doubt under pressure from Washington, who continued campaigning against this effort to organize southern black industrial schools.[63]

Holtzclaw's affiliation with ANISS did not help the faltering financial condition of Utica Institute. According to Enck, World War I had a devastating effect on black industrial schools:

Northern attention shifted to other objects of philanthropy like Belgian relief and the Red Cross. Black industrial schools were among the first to suffer. The Utica appeal for a heating plant received almost no new funds after September of 1914. By early 1915 Utica's collections for current expenses had been cut by twenty-five per cent.[64]

Holtzclaw felt an attachment to Washington that not even his school's financial exigencies could impair. Nor could the Utica principal prove ungrateful to Scott for his intercession as a fund-raiser. In the midst of his school's financial distress, Holtzclaw sent his mentor one hundred dollars "as a gift for your great work. And with the check go my earnest prayers for your continued success." Washington acknowledged his sacrifice: "Everything has been so hard this year that I am quite sure it has not been an easy matter for you to send us this large contribution, and I appreciate your kindness and thoughtfulness all the more for that reason."[65]

The ties that bound Edwards and Holtzclaw to Washington remained strong and unbreakable. Both educators owed an allegiance to their mentor, who performed as a publicist, fundraiser, advisor, and critic, providing structural supports that sustained their work. Lapses from Washington's precepts resulted in reprimand. Despite Snow Hill's financial distress, the Tuskegee founder discouraged Edwards's affiliation with ANISS. Although the evidence is scanty, there is some reason to conclude that Edwards flirted with ANISS out of economic necessity rather than from any commitment to the ideals of an anti-Washington, NAACP-inspired organization. When visitors from Tuskegee discovered Latin and German in the Snow Hill curriculum, Edwards excised these subjects immediately. There is little to suggest that the inclusion of these courses in the first place reflected an attempt to devise a curriculum that seriously deviated from the gospel of industrial education. Edwards may have been more concerned about attracting students to his normal school program than about revising his vocationally oriented program.

Edwards felt an attachment to Washington that not even the negative comments of Tuskegee visitors could impair. He simply found it impossible to meet the exacting standards of his mentor. In 1912 he wrote to Washington and noted how frustrating it was to be under his watchful eye: "I have thought of this matter very seriously. I know what my love for Tuskegee is. I try to manifest that love by being loyal to the school and by trying in an humble way to carry out its teaching. . . . Sometime, I wonder seriously what is the end that you would have us accomplish here in this school." Despite his frustration, Edwards expressed his appreciation in the very same letter: "I thank you for all you have done for me, for you have been a father to me when I had no father and all that I have done and all that I hope to do is due largely to the view of life that you instilled in me while I was in school there."[66]

Holtzclaw seemed more adept at adhering to the tenets of the Tuskegee dogma. His association with, and dependence upon, Emmett J. Scott illustrated what Louis R. Harlan has called the "octopus-like nature" of the Tuskegee Machine.[67] Described as the "general manager" of Washington's political machinations, Scott so cultivated his association with the Utica principal that Holtzclaw seemed as interested in gaining Scott's approbation as he was in pleasing Washington. As friction developed from the competition between ANISS and Washington for acceptance as the legitimate voice of southern black industrial education, Holtzclaw became a reliable cog in the Tuskegee Machine. He relished his role as a double agent. Washington's description of Scott could just as easily apply to Holtzclaw: "He has acted in the Principal's stead, seeing with the Principal's eyes and hearing with the Principal's ears, counting no sacrifice too great to be made for Tuskegee's well-being."[68]

As members of Washington's phalanx, Edwards and Holtzclaw were not free agents but "minister[s] of the Tuskegee gospel" with no allowance for wayward actions.[69] A study of Washington's relationships with both educators reveals the determination of "The Wizard of Tuskegee" to institutionalize his gospel in the black educational vanguard of Alabama and Mississippi.

Chapter Four

"Lighting a Pine Torch"

*Laurence C. Jones and the Piney Woods
Country Life School, 1909–1915*

L AURENCE C. JONES, FOUNDER OF THE
Piney Woods Country Life School in Mississippi, was neither a
southerner by birth nor a graduate of Tuskegee. He was the
product of a more favorable environment than the others in this
study. Jones was born on November 21, 1882, and raised in the
picturesque setting of St. Joseph, Missouri, "with its mills and
locomotives and steamboats trafficking in trade; its white mag-
nificent churches and schools, hotels, and parks, giving it civic
pride."[1] Jones's father, a hotel porter, was a native of Alabama,
an ex-slave who had served in the U.S. Army. His mother, a
Wisconsin native, was a seamstress. His uncle, Prior Foster,
founded the Manual Labor Institute in Addison, Michigan, in
1848, an act prophetic of what Jones was to do sixty-one years
later in Mississippi.[2]

As a youngster, Jones attended a segregated, all-black elementary school. Although Missouri did not pass segregation
laws covering public accommodations, "custom prohibited
blacks from joining whites in hotels, restaurants, theaters, and
hospitals." Jones could use the public library, but "the color of
my skin was a bar against joining or visiting the Young Men's
Christian Association" and "for billiards or pool or bowling or
checkers, the rear of some saloon was the only place open to
us."[3] Nellie Bass, Jones's sister, recalled in 1974 that "segregation was something that was accepted. Missouri was just as segregated in those days as Mississippi was just fifteen years ago."[4]

Jones left his hometown in 1898, at the age of sixteen,

seeking an "untrammeled life." He lived with relatives in Rock Island, Illinois, and in Marshalltown, Iowa. He became the first black student to graduate from Marshalltown High School in 1903. Assisted by several local white patrons and propelled by a desire for "further elevation in the mental world," the twenty-one-year-old Jones entered the University of Iowa in September of that year.[5] He studied in the College of Liberal Arts — completing courses in Latin, English literature and history — and received a Bachelor of Philosophy degree. He commented to a former teacher that "I am sure that I learned to observe closely and to classify the facts that I observed as a result of my education."[6] A talent for close observation proved to be quite an asset when he started his own school in an environment extremely different from his alma mater.

When Jones graduated in June 1907, he decided to go south. He seriously contemplated this move when he first matriculated at the University of Iowa. In a letter to the registrar in 1903, Jones stated that "I am making my own way through school and am hungary [sic] for a thorough education which I intend using in the great work of helping to elevate my race in the South." In 1911, four years after his graduation, Jones gave a newspaper reporter a different reason for his decision: "I had travelled enough through the mid-west to know how fierce competition was for people of my race who sought to establish themselves in places higher up."[7]

Jones's commitment to helping blacks in the South and his assessment of what he could or could not accomplish in the Midwest coalesced into his decision to leave Iowa. He claimed that Booker T. Washington had offered him a job at Tuskegee in the summer of 1907, but he decided instead to go to Utica Institute "because I felt that I could do the most good there."[8] He worked with William Holtzclaw as the director of the Academic Department and taught biology from 1907 to 1909. He used this opportunity to look for a school of his own, as Holtzclaw had done when he'd worked at Snow Hill Institute. Jones, however, did not have to endure the frustrations that Holtzclaw faced in finding a community that would accept his services. He was teaching in his second year at Utica when the opportunity for service came.

Jones spent Christmas of 1908 as a guest of one of his students near Braxton, twenty-five miles east of Utica, in neighboring Rankin County. A district Sunday school convention of black churches was in session, and Jones was asked to attend. He learned that black people had tried to organize a school but "no one had ever encouraged them [and] not any of them knew just what to do." Jones promised to return "to see what I could do for them."[9]

Jones fulfilled that pledge in May 1909, after he completed his term at Utica. For the next several months he trudged through Rankin County, seeking financial support for his projected school. Speaking to Sunday school associations did not bring the encouragement that Jones had received during his Christmas visit. He met with active enmity at one church gathering, finding himself "completely 'frozen out' on a sizzling August day" by church leaders "jealous of their positions as if they had been rulers of principalities." At another black church, the president of the convention, who had invited Jones to speak, was accused of bringing a "furiner" into their midst.[10] This resistance was similar to the battle over control that William J. Edwards had to wage with church officials at Snow Hill, and it contrasted sharply with the congenial relations that existed between Holtzclaw and black churches in Utica.

Jones was undaunted, however, and concluded that "the start must be made in some other way." As was his custom, he often went to read and think under the boughs of a large cedar tree. One afternoon in October 1909 he decided that "surely I ought to be able to teach these illiterate boys and girls without the formality of buildings and desks and blackboards. So the inspiration came to me to open school under the old cedar tree, with God's out-of-doors and His vast blue dome for our school house."[11]

Jones recalled that "three boys met me. . . . We assembled under the tree on some pine logs, and . . . declared school open." Near his open-air school was an old cabin owned by an ex-slave, Ed Taylor, who had once lived in Rockford, Illinois, where he had received three terms of schooling. Taylor had returned to his native Mississippi, bought some land, and become "one of the best livers in the settlement. He had more land than any other colored man around here."[12] Taylor befriended Jones, and in November 1909 he deeded to the new principal forty acres of land and his cabin for a schoolhouse. He also donated fifty dollars in cash. Jones immediately took advantage of these contributions: "We set to work, floored the old cabin, put a dirt and stick chimney to each end, and white-washed it inside and outside."[13]

Jones, a B.Phil. from the University of Iowa, thus benefited from the benevolence of an ex-slave, his first patron. At the age of twenty-seven, Jones was "happier than I had ever been before in my life." His new school was the only black private school in Rankin County and represented, at least to one of Jones's earliest students, an alternative to inadequate public schooling: "The people around in the community, they really was in favor of him [Jones] starting that school because they knew if he . . . built it up, it would be so much better to educate the children there than it was in the little . . . country schools."[14]

In this regard, the county had planned to finance a one-room school for black students with a term of three or four months and a monthly teacher's salary of between fifteen and eighteen dollars, "dependent upon the pleasure of the superintendent." Jones succeeded in convincing local black school trustees that his plans would be more beneficial, and consequently the county superintendent allowed him to receive the allocation instead of the proposed public school.[15] Jones would probably not have received this appropriation if the local black community had not distrusted the quality of public schooling available to them. His experience was not unique. Holtzclaw had used his teaching position at a public school in Utica to encourage black patronage of a private school that he wanted to build. The ability of both educators to discern and tap the self-determination of their black communities was similar.

The Piney Woods School was located "three miles from the Village of Braxton . . . in the heart of the Black Belt where the battle against ignorance and poverty must be fought in earnest."[16] Blacks comprised 59 percent of the Rankin County population in 1910.[17] The region was part of the Piney Woods, originally covered by "an unbroken expanse of long-leaf pine timber and extending over the southern half of Mississippi." The

settlers of this area came from the Carolinas and Georgia and
"by and large were not slave-owners. The relatively poor soil of
the piney woods was not conducive to profitable large-scale
farming as developed in the Delta and consequently large con-
centrations of Negroes were not found."[18] The contiguous counties of Simpson, Scott, and Smith were predominantly white, a
circumstance unlike the settings at Utica and Snow Hill. One
white visitor to Jones's school remarked that "I had never heard
of the 'piney woods' country as offering unusual attractions for
a colored school. It was supposed to be sort of a white man's
country."[19]

When Jones arrived in Mississippi in 1907, he entered a
society rife with legal, social, and educational proscriptions
(described in the previous chapter on Holtzclaw). Blacks in
Rankin County, like those in Hinds County, were not immune to
the adverse effects of poorly subsidized schooling. By 1910, in
fact, the illiteracy rate for Rankin County blacks was 51 percent, compared with only 3.9 percent for whites.[20] Jones also
labored during a time of racial violence. Eight months after he
opened his school, a black man was lynched three miles away.
During the first six years of Jones's principalship (1909–1915),
forty-eight blacks were lynched in Mississippi.[21]

The Missouri-born and Iowa-educated Jones divided southern whites into two types: "the poor illiterate ones who were
opposed to any advancement on the part of the colored man,"
and "the more prosperous, broad-minded Christian-hearted
white men, who believed in every man having a fighting chance
in life and who see in . . . negroes . . . a valuable asset to the
nation when properly educated."[22] Jones accepted the advice of
an elderly black woman who informed him that his southern
residency meant that he now had his "paw in the lion's mouth"
and cautioned him "not to be rarin' and pitchin' to get it out,"
but rather "to just ease it out the best way you can."[23] "Easing it
out" required Jones to devise strategies in order to receive benefits from "broad-minded Christian-hearted white men," while
not antagonizing "poor illiterate" whites. Since Jones's community did not have the type of planter class that Edwards of Snow
Hill relied upon, the Piney Woods educator had to depend upon
a variety of local whites for support.

One strategy Jones employed was to encourage involve-

56

ment in the affairs of his school. He boasted, for example, that the cashier of the local bank had decided to provide a "gold medal each year to the girl who made the most progress in the cooking department," and he invited the cashier's wife to judge the contestants.[24] Jones was also very interested in having local whites meet his northern visitors. A white resident remembered that Jones "had a way of bringing in big men from other places. He would frequently send me a note by a student to please come over and meet some distinguished person who was going to be there." When Jones once hosted a visitor from Iowa, he "sent out written invitations to all the white people to come. . . . There were about fifty whites there. . . . Everyone enjoyed themselves and we departed in high spirits." Jones's efforts to bring northern guests and southern white residents together did not go unnoticed by one northern visitor: "It was a great day for the principal [Jones] . . . for it brought to him the warm approval and helpful assurances of men whose endorsement of his work would give it reputation and standing throughout the country."[25]

The Piney Woods educator furthered his development of a coalition of northern and southern whites when he organized his first board of trustees in 1913. This board was comprised of two local blacks, two northern whites, and three southern whites. Jones's efforts to attract local white neighbors into the orbit of his school caused the principal of a nearby white school to remark that "to the white people of Braxton, Jones was a welcome surprise. . . . Because of his willingness to include whites in his work, his influence for good is felt by all who know him, white or black."[26] The white owner of a sawmill in Braxton remembered how well Jones, a midwesterner, had evaluated and used his tradition-bound southern surroundings: "Jones capitalized on our human weakness to want to be consulted about things. It enchanc[ed] our self-respect and satis[fied] our ego."[27]

"Messages of Hope"

When Jones started his school in the fall of 1909, only 3 students assembled "under the long leaf yellow pine trees of South Mississippi." One student remembered that "Mr. Jones had us sitting on a big long oak log and he was sitting on a little homemade stool right in front of us teaching."[28] Enrollment increased to 85 pupils a year later and reached 205 by 1915.[29]

A student who entered the school in 1910 recalled that "Piney Woods offered quite an opportunity for students who wanted to go to school and didn't have a lot of money to bare [sic] the expense. It [Piney Woods School] was in a farming section so the farmers, if they didn't have money, could pay with their produce—corn, potatoes, etc."[30] Jones discovered that many local black children wanted to attend so badly that "[students] as young as six and seven years walk four and five miles and get here by eight o'clock each morning and return the same distance each evening."[31]

Boarding students, who comprised nearly half the student body by 1915, led a hard life filled with sacrifices. Overcrowding forced some female students to sleep in the attic of their dormitory. Male students did not have a dormitory and had to sleep "in a room we finished off [in the barn], as there is no room elsewhere." Conditions worsened, and by the winter of 1913 some students slept in sheds, and "for want of mattresses, some . . . slept on boards placed on slats; some [also slept] on the floor."[32]

Forced to economize as much as possible, Jones announced that "we have been able to feed, three times a day, an average of fifty per meal at $1.50 per day. We have omitted from the bill of fare, sugar, meat and beverages and used the staples—field peas, corn bread, grits, rice, and syrup." At least one student might have complained about his diet, because his father advised in a letter, "If you can get enough of something else to eat, you must try to learn how to do without meat while you are going to school."[33]

The rigors of residential life were accentuated by Jones's insistence that his school "run smoothly like a big machine." Regular and evening bells governed the school day from 5 A.M. until 9:45 P.M.[34] Jones was no stranger to schedules since he had witnessed a similar routine when he worked at Utica Institute. The bell schedule was adopted because of Jones's belief that black students needed to cultivate certain habits because of their historical heritage: "We are just fifty years old as a free people, just children learning to walk, to catch hold on a revolving, 2000 years old civilization."[35] In Jones's view, the habits of punctuality, order, and rhythmic living were necessary devices to help students "catch hold" of their society.

No less than his contemporaries, Edwards and Holtzclaw, Jones decided to stress character building in an effort to regenerate boys and girls "ignorant of mind" and "awkward of body." He intended the Piney Woods School to be a portal of hope with clearly enunciated expectations concerning morals and manners. The "lessons for success," Jones believed, resided in such virtues as honesty, "carefulness," attentiveness, and "economy." Students could change because "their greatest asset [was] a heart yearning, craving, [and] longing for a better chance in life, for true manhood and womanhood."[36]

Some students seemed stirred by the promise of these sentiments. Although the Piney Woods School had no official graduates until 1918, there were plenty of ex-students who testified to the influence of their schooling. Aletha McClaurin, for example, thanked Jones for "providing a way for me that I may learn something." Willie Dixon reported that "you have made me have a double determination to make a man out of myself." Debbie Weathersby claimed that "I shall never forget the talks that you [gave] us every Sunday evening on trying to better our condition."[37] Parents confirmed the congruence of school and community needs. Lucy McCornell wrote that her daughter, Bertha, was "better everywhere I put her" as a result of her attendance, and Jenis McClaurin believed that the school was a "great light out of darkness. . . . A great power is coming up here in these woods." A Mrs. Magee wondered, "Where would I have been if this school wasn't here? . . . [It has sent] me messages of hope."[38]

In its effort to blaze an educational trail through the piney woods, Jones's school offered eight elementary grades and provided simple manual training in carpentry, blacksmithing, sewing, and broom-making. The Piney Woods School did not originally offer normal school training, as did Snow Hill and Utica. Formal teacher training did not appear until 1918. Instead, the liberal arts graduate from the University of Iowa decided to teach basic skills related to an agrarian life-style. A local white resident remembered that Jones "would stress the point that this was not to be a book larnin' school." Pupils above the sixth grade attended classes four days and worked two days a week. Courses were, in Jones's words, "stripped of every educational frill. We do not try to teach these boys and girls who are to live in the country, an education for city life."[39]

The largest white daily newspaper in Mississippi discovered distinct social and racial connotations in the curriculum. The *Jackson Daily News* believed that black people should be trained "as a country people. It is best for them [and] best for the white man." Opposed to black migration to the North, the paper applauded Jones for "leading his people right . . . [by] teaching them that the surest happiness and contentment will come to any man who knows how to properly farm." Jones never openly challenged the message of this endorsement. Indeed, he argued tenaciously throughout the period that blacks must remain "country-folk" and that this status did not stifle aspirations or ambitions.[40] The opposite was true. Blacks could build "better schools and be more consistent Christians" in the rural South, away from the temptations and evils of city life.[41]

Jones did not have to spread the "light of industry and intelligence" by himself. Although he opened his school as the only teacher, he was soon joined by two of his former students at Utica Institute. They completed their first year without salaries.[42] Piney Woods opened its second year in October 1910 with five teachers, including Louis Watson, a young man who had met Jones when the new principal had made his first fund-raising trip to Iowa the previous summer. Watson completed high school in Des Moines and worked as a porter before casting his lot in Mississippi.

Jones found another black Iowa resident in 1911 when he met William Franklin Reden. Reden had received a law degree from the University of Iowa in 1908 but could not find employment. Reden decided "to enter the work like the rest of us without regard to salary." A year later Jones married Grace Morris Allen, a native of Burlington, Iowa, and a former student at the Chicago Conservatory of Music. She took charge of the domestic science department.[43] Three of the six teachers at Piney Woods in the fall of 1912 had educational roots in Iowa, a background very different from the Tuskegee-dominated staffs at Snow Hill and Utica. Teachers were selected for their ability "to teach not only books but some industrial subject, so that they are found in the shop or field when not in the school room. . . . In this way everybody . . . [is] busy from the rising . . . until the retiring bell."[44]

The Piney Woods School was designed to be a positive force in the community and was consistently advertised as a "Center of Extention [sic] Education."[45] Although he did not develop projects as ambitious as Edwards's and Holtzclaw's Black Belt Improvement Societies, Jones sponsored farmers' conferences and attempted to make his school an "object lesson" for local farmers.[46] Piney Woods lacked the resources of its Tuskegee counterparts, and consequently Jones conducted a large amount of extension work by mail, sending the following message to those he could not reach through personal contact:

LOOKING FORWARD

Do you want to continue to stand still? Why not awaken? You can do better. Then why not? Pledge yourselve [sic] to help make at least one improvement upon your church and school house. Pledge yourselve [sic] to make some improvement upon your home.[47]

Jones assiduously tried to obtain financial support for his instructional and extension activities by conducting "Northern Campaigns"—appeals for help and trips north in search of funds. His initial effort to raise money did not fare well. He sent out one thousand written appeals in the winter of 1909 but received only one response of fifteen dollars.[48] His concern for his school took him to his adopted state of Iowa the following summer, where he solicited first in Keokuk. There he discovered some broom-making machinery on sale for thirty-five dollars. It took him a week to raise that amount. He next went to Des Moines, where a fellow black alumnus of the University of Iowa arranged a meeting in a white church. Not many attended, but Jones "raised a little money [and] secured some pledges."[49]

Efforts to raise money in the Des Moines black community were significantly assisted in 1911 by publicity in the *Des Moines Iowa State Bystander,* a black-owned weekly. This paper issued a challenge to blacks: "Show your color. This is a test. The opportunity is yours." Calling Jones "one of our own boys" and celebrating his "sacrifice and labor," the *Bystander* urged "every church women's club, missionary society, and literary organization to join this movement . . . by sending from a dollar up." Jones raised one hundred dollars through this appeal, "enough . . . to buy a horse, wagon, farm tools, winter clothing for the teachers and to pay some small bills."[50] This was not the only occasion that Piney Woods received sustenance from black Iowans. In 1914 the A. P. I. Club of Sioux City, "an organization of colored Ladies," sent clothing, and a black woman donated her property to the school.[51]

The task of traveling to raise funds was often fraught with difficulties for Jones. Not the least of his problems resulted from the racial discrimination that he faced in the Midwest. He once lamented that "the pathway of a colored man who would help solve the problem of industrially educating . . . colored Americans is by no means always pleasant . . . when your skin is the wrong color." Jones had difficulty in finding lodging in "fair Iowa" because, as he wrote, "hotels are generally 'full' if a colored person wishes to sleep." The hostility that he faced in the Midwest caused the Piney Woods principal "whenever . . . possible to find my own people . . . and it was always as a last resort that I risk[ed] going elsewhere."[52]

In addition to his travels, Jones reached supporters through his monthly newsletter, *The Pine Torch,* first printed in May 1911. The list of basic school "needs" was constantly advertised: "1. Agricultural papers and magazines. 2. Clothing of any kind for needy, but worthy students. 3. Money in small or large sums for current expenses."[53] Jones acknowledged receiving books from New Haven, Connecticut; farm journals from Philadelphia; and printing supplies from Minnesota.[54] Patrons in Iowa contributed most frequently: cash from Marshalltown and Mason City, a typewriter and a mower rake from Des Moines, Sunday school materials from Iowa City, and magazines from Clinton.[55]

Jones did not have a Booker T. Washington to act as an intermediary for donations, as did Edwards and Holtzclaw, nor did he reap advantages from the publicity that Washington gained for his graduates. He did not receive philanthropic support from 1909 to 1915.[56] Jones did not benefit from a close association with a wealthy local patron and did not speak before

Tuskegee audiences. His focus differed from that of those educators within the circuit of Tuskegee. While Edwards and Holtzclaw traveled to Boston and New York City, Jones cultivated a Piney Woods constituency in Iowa by "walking the hard pavements day after day in the sweltering sun or cutting winds and blinding snows" of Keokuk, Marshalltown, and Des Moines.[57]

After five years of serving as principal, Jones reflected that his school did not have "any ancient traditions, classic memories, or [a] long list of achievements." Instead, Piney Woods was a "simple, country life school which will carry the gospel of . . . better living, better schools and churches to those who live back from the main-traveled roads." Jones viewed his constituency as "a good strong hardy people who have never had a real chance in life."[58]

He had come to Rankin County alone from nearby Utica. Nobody had sent him. He had no substantial backers. But this "colored Yankee" managed to garner local black support after encountering confusion and disarray. One black supporter admitted that when Jones arrived "we was watching him [but] ever time we'd set a trigger fer him he . . . jest stepped [out] of it to one side."[59] He was equally skilled at cultivating whites in his community.

Unlike the other black educators in this study, Jones was a southerner by adoption and not by birth. He readily adjusted to his racially constricted environment and celebrated the virtues of an agrarian life as enthusiastically as any Tuskegee progeny. With far fewer resources than his counterparts at Snow Hill and Utica, Jones chose "Character and Service" as the crucible of advancement for his people.[60]

THE PINEY WOODS SCHOOL AFTER 1915: Laurence C. Jones retired in 1974, after serving sixty-five years as principal. He died at the age of ninety-two a year later. Teacher training became part of the curriculum in 1918, and a two-year junior college program was established in 1931 (it was discontinued in the 1960s). The school is presently a coeducational boarding institution for the first through twelfth grades.

Chapter Five

"An Educator and an Humble Christian Worker"

*Thomas O. Fuller and Howe Institute,
1900–1915*

T HOMAS O. FULLER CAME TO MEMPHIS, Tennessee, in 1900 as a minister, but two years later he was selected principal of Howe Institute, a Baptist school founded in 1888. An analysis of Fuller's leadership provides a case study of how one black educator applied his southern urban environment to the "fortunes of [his] race," while his contemporaries at Snow Hill, Utica, and Piney Woods labored in the shadows of the plantation.

Fuller was born in North Carolina on October 25, 1867, in Franklinton, twenty-seven miles north of Raleigh, the state capitol. The youngest of fourteen children born to former slaves, Fuller remembered his parents as "old time Christians, of deep piety and consecrated common sense, though uneducated in books."[1] Fuller attended a private school for blacks at age five, where "the three 'R's' had the right-of-way." He matriculated at a state normal school for black students that opened in his hometown in 1882; he was a member of the first class. Admission requirements allowed "any Negro youth between fifteen and twenty-five who was able to pass a good examination in reading, spelling, writing, and the fundamental rules of arithmetic to enroll for training."[2] Fuller graduated from the Franklinton Normal School for Negroes in 1885, and in that same year—at the age of eighteen—he entered Shaw University in Raleigh.

Shaw University was founded in 1865 by a white Baptist clergyman from Massachusetts and chartered in 1875 for the training of the Baptist ministry, the first college for black Baptists in North Carolina.[3] Fuller described his college days as "both interesting and eventful" but not without struggle. His limited resources made it necessary for him to work to meet school and living expenses. While the future educator was "trained for service" at Shaw, he participated in a mission Sunday school, where "I gathered many idle children from the streets of the city and placed them under the instruction of volunteer teachers who gave them a rich foretaste of the better life."[4] In May 1890 Fuller received his bachelor of arts degree and became one of only ninety-five blacks who completed a four-year college education in the United States that year. He received his M.A. from Shaw in 1893 and was ordained a minister the same year.[5]

Fuller began his career as a teacher in 1890 in a black public school in Granville County. At the request of Baptists in his hometown of Franklinton, he founded the Girl's Training School in 1892. He remained there for two years before moving to Warren County and becoming principal of another black Baptist school, Shiloh Institute, in Warrenton.[6] Black Baptists were attracted to private schooling not only because of religious motivation but because "the poorly-housed, inadequately-supported, meagerly-equipped public schools did not offer opportunities in quite the measure that Negroes were seeking."[7] Public schooling for blacks in Warren County was no exception: "The negro schoolhouses are packed like sardine boxes scarcely giving comfortable standing room, much less sitting room. What can the most competent teacher do in such a howling wilderness?"[8]

Fuller remained at Shiloh until 1898, when he was elected to the North Carolina legislature for one term as its only black senator. His role as a politician was not, he claimed, the result of a long-cherished aspiration. A vacancy occurred on the Republican ticket in the predominantly black Eleventh Senatorial District, and Fuller accepted the nomination only after "being assured that I would be relieved from making campaign speeches.

. . . I was a school principal and pastor and didn't care to mix politics with the situation."[9] The election of 1898 was bitterly contested by Democrats in North Carolina who launched a white supremacy campaign and gained control of the state legislature. Fuller did not envision his new role as a protest against the white Democratic blacklash. He reminded his constituents before he took his seat that "I am not a politican nor do I pose as your political leader. It is well known that I am an educator and an humble Christian worker. . . . I shall DEMAND nothing."[10]

Taking office in the wake of extreme racial tension, Fuller felt like a "leaf in a hurricane." He was denied committee assignments but managed to sponsor legislation relating to temperance and county courts. In 1900, a year after he completed his work in the senate, Fuller accepted a call from a black Baptist church in Memphis, Tennessee. The chance to become a pastor in a large city excited him, and the challenge of building a new church inspired him even more. At the age of thirty-three, Fuller left his native North Carolina where he had been educated, and helped to establish two schools, pastored numerous churches, and served a brief tenure in politics. He was "off to Tennessee."[11]

Although Fuller came to Memphis to preach, he was asked in 1901 to teach a course in religion to a class of ministers at Howe Institute, an elementary-secondary school owned and operated by black Baptists. He gained favorable publicity for his efforts in the *Memphis Commercial Appeal:* "The theological class of Howe Institute was fortunate this year to secure the services of the Rev. T. O. Fuller, a graduate of Shaw University. Too much can not be said commendatory of the faithful services of Rev. Fuller, who has already been a blessing to Memphis." A local black educator remembered that Fuller brought to his teaching a "skillful technical training resulting from a thorough college education, a facility of execution, a clearness of exposition, a brilliant rhetorical display, and an astonishing erudition which simply overwhelmed and swept everything before him."[12]

When a vacancy in the principalship at Howe occurred in 1902, the board of trustees offered the position to Fuller, who accepted and pledged to *"make it hum."*[13] The school had received its start when a group of black Baptist ministers in Memphis, without land or buildings, initiated a "center of moral and religious influence" in the Tabernacle Baptist Colored Church. The pastor of this church sought funds in the North and found a benefactor named Howe in Illinois, enabling the founders to build a "large, commodious, three-story brick building." The school offered elementary and secondary instruction within a religious context.[14]

When Fuller assumed his new duties, Howe Institute was encumbered with "embarrassing debts" and a dilapidated building. These conditions had "alienated many of the best and most loyal members of the denomination." Fuller remembered that "things looked dark." However, the new principal was not a novice. He had previously built two schools and had worked with groups of black churches that financially supported education. His was an important responsibility since Howe was the only institution operated by his denomination in Memphis and one of only three in that city to offer secondary education to blacks.[15]

Fuller is the only black educator in this study who lived and worked in an urban setting. The black population of Memphis in 1870 was 15,471; by 1900, the year that Fuller arrived, it had increased to 59,910, which amounted to 48.8 percent of the total population. Only five cities in America had larger black populations. Most of these new black residents were part of a "swelling tide of immigrants from the countryside of West Tennessee, Mississippi, and Arkansas."[16] This migration might have been responsible for elevating the black clergy to positions of community leadership in Memphis during the 1900s. According to historian Lester C. Lamon, rural migrants were in "the habit of looking to black clergymen for social, economic, and political guidance." Black ministers assumed important community roles because Memphis did not have a significant black middle class: "Lack of strong community ties and constant mobility left Memphis without black civic, business, and social clubs. Consequently, black leaders . . . were more often ministers." Historian David M. Tucker has concurred, concluding that the black clergy in Memphis exercised influence and "became dominant in the black community."[17]

Fuller was fully aware of this opportunity for leadership

and status. He once told a group of black Memphis ministers that "the Negro preacher needs to know how to utilize the various elements of strength about him." The Howe Institute principal certainly did not neglect the benefits of his own social position. He became president of the Mount Carmel Cemetery, a company that was organized in 1909 and capitalized at sixty thousand dollars.[18] Fuller also became one of the largest realtors in Memphis with a business portfolio of "nearly sixty pieces of improved and unimproved property."[19]

When he arrived in Tennessee, Fuller entered a racially divided society. A series of restrictions on suffrage had virtually disenfranchised black voters, and the Tennessee legislature passed a law in 1901 that prevented students in private institutions from being taught by a member of a different race. Memphis adhered to segregation; public schools, residential neighborhoods, theaters, and parks were all segregated. According to one historian, white people in Memphis "still looked to the past, to the old South, for their ideals. Of these . . . the most passionately upheld was that of white supremacy. It was held above religion, morality, or law."[20]

White supremacy received a ringing affirmation in the *Memphis Commercial Appeal*. When the Boston Women's Club admitted black women members in 1900, the paper called it a "coon club composed of negresses and degenerate white women." Readers were advised that "the Anglo-Saxon will not be ruled no matter what the odds are against him. He possesses that imperious and unyielding despotism of conscious superiority." When Theodore Roosevelt had Booker T. Washington to lunch at the White House in 1901, the paper labeled the president a "flute player and tin cowboy" who had turned the White House into a "nigger restaurant." Despite Washington's accomplishments, he was still "an Alabama coon."[21]

How did Fuller respond to this racial climate? His first documented response occurred in 1905. In March of that year the Tennessee legislature passed a law segregating passengers on streetcars, effective July 5. The *Commercial Appeal* supported the new law because "there can be no doubt that many of the negroes who travel on streetcars are offensive to the white passengers. It is the conduct of these creatures that has aroused sentiment against the negro generally."[22] Although a black man was arrested in July for sitting in the section assigned to whites and another was ejected from a streetcar for doing the same thing in August, Fuller refused to protest the new law. Instead, in a letter to the *Commercial Appeal,* he instructed blacks to respect the law and obey the conductors, "whose position under the circumstances, is both trying and hazardous." His position was prompted "by my duty as a citizen of Memphis, having religious, educational and property interests that demand the most peaceable conditions and the most perfect harmony and cooperation between the races that can be secured."[23]

Fuller's public acquiescence to racial restrictions was not suddenly developed in Memphis. He had decided when he was elected to the North Carolina Senate in 1898 that he would not offer protest leadership. He brought his conservatism to Tennessee and regarded the cultivation of friendships with leading white citizens a "very, very wise thing on the part of a [black] man." While others planned "mischief," he embraced a "carefulness of speech" and "tactful patience."[24] As a principal and preacher, he "elevated racial adjustment to a major ministerial art." He did not do this alone, however. A "conservative accommodationism" characterized the "entire black ministerial leadership" of Memphis and hindered protest.[25] Fuller seemed convinced that his racial strategy was appropriate: "In the Southland, where the warp and woof of the social fabric are not complicated, discretion is most essential . . . if a colored man is to lead his people without friction in the paths of wisdom, peace, happiness, and prosperity."[26]

"Sparks from Many Anvils"

Within the confines of a racially tense community, Fuller sought to reverse the declining conditions of Howe Institute that he inherited in 1902. He proudly reported two years later that student enrollment had reached 241, "the largest attendance in our history." In 1905 he informed the *Commercial Appeal* that registration had reached 301. Ten years later (1915) the school reported an enrollment of 270.[27]

Despite its urban location, Howe Institute primarily served a rural student body. Fifty-one percent of the students by 1913 came from agrarian communities in western Tennessee, eastern Arkansas, and northern Mississippi. Visitors in 1915 noted the school's "large constituency among the Baptists of the surrounding country districts."[28] The rural origins of his students prompted Fuller's concern for their character development (a concern shared by his counterparts at Snow Hill, Utica, and Piney Woods). Urban life created "menacing and hazardous" conditions, he believed, with its "dives and dens where criminals are bred and crime is hatched." He railed against the "educated idler" who posed a "menace to society and a danger to civilization."[29]

Consequently, students at Howe had to follow a strict daily routine. All students were expected "to be in their seats in the chapel each morning before the 9 o'clock bell strikes . . . [and] quiet and respectful deportment will be required at all times." Students were to dress "neatly but not extravagantly," and a "modest uniform" was required for female students: "Navy blue tailored suits for winter wear, white shirtwaists with blue skirts for early fall and spring wear. College caps in the winter and sailor hats in the spring." Naturally, religious life was not neglected. Students had to identify themselves with some church and attend "[a] religious service at least once every Sunday." The school offered a weekly prayer meeting, and every Friday evening Howe students assembled to discuss a Sunday school lesson.[30] Fuller was particularly proud of the "Soul-saving Meetings" presided over by his wife in the church that he pastored, conveniently located across the street from the school. He claimed that at these gatherings "scores of students, many of them on the eve of graduation, have been made to 'Know Christ.' "[31]

Female students who needed to work to pay expenses at first were not permitted to do so away from the school because of Fuller's belief that housing and protection in urban Memphis were inadequate. He later relented and allowed his female pupils to work "at places approved by the Principal." No such sanctions applied to male students. By 1909, 70 percent of these students worked as servants in the homes "of the best [white] people of Memphis," earning room, board, and ten dollars a month.[32]

Tuition at Howe cost $1.25 a month for students in the first five grades and $1.50 a month for those enrolled above the fifth grade. Boarding students — few in number due to lack of facilities — paid a monthly fee of $9. Evidently, these charges were not easily met, because 60 percent of the entire student body was earning its way through school by 1909.[33]

Fuller believed that graduates of his school had "no false notions of life. They have been taught to believe in the dignity of labor." Indeed, when compared with alumni of an earlier time, a compelling change in employment appears to have occurred for those students who graduated after Fuller became principal in 1902. Seventy-seven students officially graduated between 1891 and 1903, and the occupations of 46 (60 percent) were listed in a 1913 school catalog. Twenty-two (48 percent) of this group were teachers; 11 (24 percent) were lawyers, dentists, or physicians; and 5 (11 percent) were ministers. Only 4 alumni listed nonprofessional careers: 2 seamstresses, 1 printer, and 1 domestic.[34]

A different kind of graduate emerged after ten years of Fuller's leadership. Howe graduated 231 students between 1904 and 1912, and the status of 175 was known. Of this group, 118 (67 percent) completed their studies in stenography, typing, and sewing. Only 50 (22 percent) pursued an academic course.[35] Fuller was not bashful about claiming credit for such a change in his school's direction. In 1909 he informed the *Commercial Appeal* that prior to his arrival visitors found "some good Latin and Greek exercises on the blackboard . . . but the windows were dim with dirt and the trades and domestic sciences were not in evidence. It is the intention of the present principal to elaborate on the industrial features."[36] Fuller's reference to Latin and Greek amidst windows "dim with dirt" resembled Booker T. Washington's assertion in *Up from Slavery* that "one of the saddest things I saw (as a principal) was a young man, who had attended some high school, sitting down in a one-room cabin, with grease on his clothing, filth all around him, and weeds in the yard and garden, engaged in studying a French grammar."[37]

From its founding in 1888 until 1902, Howe Institute offered eight elementary and three secondary grades with no "industrial features." Fuller intended to develop industrial education and to keep intact the liberal arts aspect of the curriculum that he had inherited. In 1905 he reported that "an urgent priority is a faculty for Manual and Industrial Training. Our people must work and training that better fits them for honest toil is a blessing."[38] Domestic training for female students received an important boost when a new dormitory for women was completed in 1909. The new facility contained a "kitchen, laundry, ironing room and [a] model dining-room," and "all [female students were] expected to enroll in the domestic science classes [since] the equipment is exceptionally fine for such work." The Memphis Consolidated Gas and Electric Company equipped a room in the new building with gas ranges free of charge and even provided a "demonstrator . . . to teach all the girls the use of [this equipment]." Fuller decided to make the most of this patronage and publicly invited "any Negro cook in Memphis who wishes to know how to operate her mistress' gas range . . . to come . . . and learn, free of charge, any and all things needful."[39]

Howe Institute now became a demonstration center where black female secondary students could receive "practical instruction in economic cooking" from members of various "Housekeepers Clubs," who appeared before the student body "to offer suggestions as to what is expected of a good, well-equipped domestic."[40] Female students could also choose to enroll in certification programs in sewing, millinery, stenography, and typing.

Howe Institute also wanted to train "the hands . . . of her dusky sons," but the school never managed to build a well-equipped industrial shop between 1902 and 1915. Fuller had announced plans in 1905 for his male students to study carpentry, bricklaying, and painting, but manual training remained limited to printing. Visitors to the school in 1914 found existing equipment to be inadequate.[41] Fuller had not received the financial patronage needed to expand the curriculum for males in the same way that he did for female students. Perhaps the fact that more male alumni graduated from the Academic rather than the Manual Training Department affected Fuller's success in developing industrial courses. It is also possible that male students were attracted to Howe because of its ministerial program and not its vocational features.

Industrial training at Howe was offered only to students who had completed the eighth grade. Students in the first through the fifth grades were offered a "thorough beginning in the rudiments," and those in grades six through eight continued their study of "Practical Arithmetic," reading, spelling, grammar, and composition. All nonvocational students in grades nine through eleven were required to study mathematics and English for three years and history for two years. Ministerial candidates also could study a year of Latin and Greek.[42]

Although enrollment in basic courses always exceeded that of the industrial offerings, Fuller never publicized the academic programs in the interviews he gave to local reporters. He spoke instead of industrial training. David Tucker maintains that this was a deliberate and prudent strategy to gain support from whites, who wanted black cooks rather than scholars. Historian August Meier likewise has contended that often industrial education at black schools bought "Southern good will."[43] Although the urban setting of Howe Institute contrasted vividly with the rual environments in which the other three black educators in this study worked, Fuller adjusted as well to the political and racial constraint of his surroundings. He seemed to fit as comfortably into the ambience of Memphis as the others did into their respective milieus.

Fuller inherited two restrictions on the kind of faculty members that he could hire. The school's charter stipulated that teachers had to be upright Christians, and a Tennessee law prohibited racially mixed staffs at private schools. The faculty at Howe, therefore, had to be black and Christian, preferably Baptist. Fuller reported an "all colored" staff of ten in 1905, and that number had increased to fourteen ten years later. The number of teachers in the Academic Department far exceeded those who taught manual training. In fact, only three teachers taught nonacademic courses by 1915. Fuller used Howe graduates and those from another Baptist-affiliated school, Roger Williams University in Nashville, as the main sources for his faculty. A third of the staff in 1908 graduated from Howe, and three more were alumni of the Baptist school in Nashville. Eleven of the twelve faculty members in that year were graduates of black private, church-affiliated schools in the South; only one graduate was from a northern school.[44]

As he built his school, Fuller became interested in extending its influence into the black community. His approach, however, was different from the others in this study and reflected the religious nature of his school. There were no farmers' conferences or Black Belt Improvement Societies at Howe Institute. Instead, Fuller expanded the Women's Bible Training Class (WBTC) and two extension activities that had existed before he became the principal.

The WBTC gained considerable impetus when seventy-five "colored women, their ages ranging from 25 to 55, and nearly all of them married," accepted Fuller's invitation "to follow a special course of *Bible* study at no cost" in 1904. The class met daily at Howe Institute for two hours from January to March. Attendance reportedly reached 217, from "thirty churches and seven denominations," by 1913.[45]

The class combined *Bible* study with self-improvement. Lessons emphasized "individual purity, consecration of life for the uplift of others, [and] the organization and development of [a] well-ordered home life." Fuller claimed that he witnessed the transformation of some of his adult female students, because "many . . . were known to lay aside certain habits of life and the use of snuff, tobacco and beverages as they learned their injurious effects." It was his hope that changed women would lead to changed children. WBTC participants were encouraged to become agents of reform and missionaries to the "poor neglected children of their neighborhoods," who need to learn to be "thoughtful, careful, and helpful to their neighbors."[46]

After a systematic course of *Bible* instruction, WBTC women were also expected to help the pastors of their respective churches. But their assistance was not always welcome. One minister, alarmed that women were studying the *Bible* "so thoroughly," reportedly asked one of the participants if she intended to preach. " 'No,' she replied, 'but we shall learn so much about the *Bible* that nobody can preach to us but a preacher.' " Fuller recalled that his training class students were "teaching the *Bible* in their churches . . . and so enlightening the masses that the demand for a better prepared ministry is steadily increasing."[47]

The other extension effort at Howe was a weekly ministerial training class designed to meet the needs of clergy in the "active pastorate." Fuller taught church history and theology and helped his class prepare sermon outlines. This last feature proved, according to Fuller, "quite a drawing card. . . . The ministers went to their pulpits on Sunday with a fresh, live message and their congregations were delighted and were so free in expressing their approval . . . that the pastor found it necessary to continue studying."[48]

Fuller's direct involvement with his school's extension efforts was matched only by his prodigious efforts to raise funds for his school. Howe Institute was staggering under a great debt when he became principal. A restriction in the 1888 school charter stipulated that no money could be raised by "fairs, festivals, suppers, excursions, or by advertising any articles of trade or business." This limitation forced the school to rely upon black field agents to raise money. Fuller inherited, then, initial northern support from the school's original benefactors, the Howe family, and black self-help.[49]

Fuller informed a local newspaper in 1905 that his school depended upon tuition and donations from "Negro churches, associations, and individuals." The expense of running Howe for 1905–6 was $4,000. Tuition amounted to $1,750 — 44 percent of the total budget. Black churches in Tennessee contributed $1,630 — accounting for 41 percent — and the remaining $620 came from the American Baptist Home Mission Society (ABHMS) of New York City. For 1905–6, then, support from black people comprised 85 percent of the budget.[50] Black financial support continued to account for the largest share of the Howe Institute budget as the 1900s progressed. By the school year 1909–10, contributions from black churches and individuals ($2,844), added to the amount received from tuition ($2,650), comprised 89 percent of the $6,125 budget. Considering these figures, it was perhaps understandable for Fuller to praise the "forty-three Negro churches of this faith (Baptist) in Memphis, with its 10,000 members, and the others throughout the state who see that money is raised for the school when needed."[51]

Fuller skillfully enlisted the cooperation of both black Baptists in Tennessee and northern philanthropy in developing the campus of his school from one building in 1902 to four by 1910. He asked the Baptist Young People's Union (BYPU) of Memphis, an organization of local black Baptist youth, to inaugurate a "spendid financial rally" that resulted in the BYPU Industrial Shop. This building provided room for "printing, sewing, and laundry departments" [and was] our maiden effort at enlargement." When Fuller decided that the school needed a building to serve as both a dormitory for females and a domestic science building, he asked the General Education Board (GEB), established by John D. Rockefeller, for assistance. The GEB appropriated $3,000 for Howe Institute in 1907, provided "we raise[d] a like amount and that it would be paid thousand for thousand . . . so that the work of the building could go forward." This support "cheered the Baptists of West Tennessee to a high pitch of enthusiasm. Ministers, churches, missionary societies and individuals caught the spirit and rallied to our support." Fuller raised the $3,000 needed to match the GEB grant in one year.[52]

When the combined Girls' Dormitory and Domestic Science Building, a "three-story, concrete and brick veneer building," was completed in the fall of 1909, Fuller persuaded several local black churches to furnish each room. The Women's Auxiliary of the West Tennessee (Baptist) Association furnished the reception room in "royal style," and the St. John Church outfitted one of the bedrooms "in beautiful fashion." Faculty members raised money by giving concerts, and "several of the 'grades' of the school . . . made gifts of supplies and money which helped us no little in the struggle." The WBTC had pledged to donate at least a dollar for each member toward the dormitory-classroom building, and each one agreed "to earn the money by some special work or deny herself of some comfort." Fuller described the WBTC commitment thus: "Some earned their money by 'patching,' selling lye, hominy and scaly barks, 'laundry work,' selling literature, walking miles to the class and saving car fare, selling pies, and many other ways." These donations constituted "self-denial money." At the same time that the new building was completed, the "Teachers' Cottage" (the name given to the home of the principal) was also built.[53]

There were some important differences between the fund-raising activities of Fuller and the efforts to raise money by the other black educators in this study. There is no evidence, for instance, that Fuller received money for his school from any secular northern philanthropy other than the General Education Board. He mainly relied upon the religious affiliation of his school for his funds. On the other hand, William J. Edwards benefited from his association with Washington: as an offshoot of Tuskegee, Snow Hill Institute received grants from the Slater and the Rosenwald funds as well as a donation of ten thousand dollars from Andrew Carnegie. Holtzclaw also received financial support for his school as a result of his fraternity with Washington and Emmett J. Scott. Jones, however, received no money from a philanthropic source during the first years (1909–15) of his principalship.

Fuller's constituency of "various Negro Baptist churches, clubs, societies, and individuals" put his school "on a substantial working basis," according to one Memphis observer. Fuller also had status in the community as the pastor of a church with a reported membership of 350, the fifth largest of forty-three black Baptist churches in the city in 1908. One contemporary remembered that Fuller was "in great demand upon all demonstrative occasions."[54] Fuller's ministerial status was as crucial to his fund-raising efforts as Edwards's and Holtzclaw's Tuskegee affiliation was to theirs.

G. P. Hamilton, principal of a public high school for black students in Memphis during the 1900s, considered the selection of Fuller as principal of Howe Institute "the great turning point in the life of that school . . . [which] seemed to have fallen on evil days. Fuller's taking hold of the reins of authority at that crucial time was the beginning of better days for the school."[55] Howe Institute did change between 1902 and 1915. The school plant increased from one to four buildings. The original three-story Howe Building stood "like a sentinel on the corner of the campus." Nearby were the Domestic Science-Dormitory facility for female students, the industrial shop, and Fuller's home. These properties comprised one-fourth of a city block. Fuller had adeptly used the financial support offered by his black Baptist brethren to expand his campus.

Fuller assumed responsibility for a school that had provided elementary and secondary education but no industrial
training since its founding in 1888. The B.A. graduate, an
"alumnus of the classical department of Shaw University," decided to graft cooking, printing, and stenography onto the liberal arts core of his school. This decision gained him the approbation of many whites, especially the local press. He made the
most of this approval and, according to Tucker, "spent much of
his time meeting with white politicians, businessmen, and editors." His educational aims were perceived by one white newspaper as "practical and sane."[56]

But white sanction was perhaps more a result of, than a
cause for, the introduction of manual training courses at Howe.
Fuller believed that black people were "in the morning of [their]
greatness" and held the "key" to the industrial development of
the South as the region's "choicest laborer[s]." Industrial education, therefore, did not mean subservience but "intelligent citi-
zenship [and] trained labor."[57] Fuller really endeavored to make
the most of his southern urban setting, and he joined Edwards,
Holtzclaw, and Jones as satellites in a black educational firma-
ment dominated by the constellation of Booker T. Washington.

HOWE INSTITUTE AFTER 1915: Thomas Fuller remained principal of Howe Institute until 1931. He
turned to the writing of black history and published
The Pictorial History of the American Negro (1933)
and *The History of the Negro Baptist of Tennessee*
(1936). Howe Institute closed in 1937, and Fuller
died in 1942 at the age of seventy-five.

Chapter Six
Conclusion

THE HISTORY OF THESE FOUR BLACK
educators and the schools that they founded and served demonstrates that contemporary political, economic, and cultural conditions directly influenced the development of educational policy. The milieu of black school leadership dictated that certain perspectives, methodologies, and associations would remain constant in the southern black experience. The choices these educators made and the challenges they encountered influenced the basic orientation of each institution.

In the very act of establishing their schools, the four educators faced a variety of obstacles within the black community. Edwards faced opposition from black parents who resisted industrial education as well as antagonism from his church over jurisdiction of Snow Hill Institute. Even though Edwards started his school in his own community, he cautiously and deliberately studied his locale before beginning his work. Holtzclaw had to travel to Mississippi four times before he could even find a community receptive to his plans. Jones, encouraged at first by local blacks to come to the piney woods, encountered confusion, inertia, and opposition from this same sector upon his arrival. The initial proving ground, then, for three of the educators was located amidst friction within their black constituencies. The viability, endurance, and strength of black educational leadership had to be tested first in black society.

Sustaining their schools proved as formidable a task as starting them, and the obstacles were almost insuperable. Edwards and Holtzclaw were never able to develop viable manual training facilities, and few of their students actually graduated. Resources for Jones were even more limited, and Fuller did not successfully devise an industrial curriculum beyond cooking and printing. Boarding students at Utica and the Piney Woods School endured particularly harsh life-styles. Fund-raising for Edwards, Holtzclaw, and Jones proved arduous and often unrewarding. Although Fuller's black Baptist supporters eventually sustained Howe Institute, he inherited an institution ravaged by decay and deterioration.

Beyond these impediments, however, lay a hardening determination to establish and nurture schools for black students by any means necessary. Holtzclaw and Jones took advantage of local black distrust of public schooling. The Utica principal used his initial position in a public school to build support for a private one; the Piney Woods educator, with black support, received money appropriated for a public school. Fuller added an industrial education component to the liberal arts core of Howe Institute, enabling the school to gain much-needed support from local authorities while preserving its academic mission. These educators had to be initiators and reactors, inaugurators and respondents. They no doubt would have recognized themselves in Edwards's portrayal of the black educator: "He finds no way prepared, he must make one; he finds no school-house ready, he must build one; he finds no people anxiously awaiting him, he must persuade them."[1]

The educational leadership provided by Edwards and Holtzclaw was significantly influenced by their affiliation with Booker T. Washington, who publicized their schools and helped them gain access to philanthropic sources. But progenies of Tuskegee were captives of the Tuskegee Machine rather than free agents. Strict adherence to the Tuskegee gospel was a virtue, whereas deviation — as Edwards discovered — was a vice. The influence of Washington on Jones and Fuller was far less direct. Jones appeared personally aloof from Tuskegee and the praise offered to Washington by his fellow black educators. He sought his faculty in the Midwest and cultivated fund-raising sources in Iowa. He claimed that he refused an offer to teach at Tuskegee. Although Jones worked in the shadow of Washington's example and certainly advocated industrial education, he probably exercised more independence from outside forces when tending to the educational needs of his community, than did his peers when tending to theirs.

Fuller publicly expressed admiration for the Tuskegee principal in several speeches, offered an encomium in his autobiography, and visited Tuskegee at least once between 1900 and 1910.[2] But the denominational status of Howe Institute caused Fuller to seek funds from black Baptists with no reliance upon Washington. Nor did Fuller depend upon Tuskegee for faculty, appearing content to staff his institution with his own graduates and those from other church-affiliated schools.

However, despite Fuller's personal independence from Tuskegee, it would be a mistake not to mention the appeal that Washington had for a rising black middle class in the urban South. According to historian August Meier, Washington's advocacy of industrial education and his emphasis upon industry and thrift appealed especially to "self-made middle-class Negroes in the South, to the leaders and supporters of Negro fraternal enterprises, and to businessmen who depended on the Negro community for their livelihood." Fuller belonged to a small middle class in Memphis with vested business interests, and it was this class, "composed of men whose economic roots were in the newly urbanized masses . . . [that] naturally found the educational philosophy of self-help congenial to its experience and interests."[3] Although it is easier to discern the extent to which Washington directly and personally influenced Edwards and Holtzclaw, the prestige of the Tuskegee founder definitely had an impact on Fuller, reinforcing, if not helping to initiate, his educational approach.

The development of the policies and practices of these educators can also be analyzed within the context of the three Rs: race, ruralism, and reformation. Each educator by necessity became a racial tactician, forced to plot strategies and to display a repertoire of responses in order to survive his racially divided environment. The flames of racism burned brightly in Alabama, Mississippi, and Tennessee by 1900. Black people were politically disenfranchised, and many lived in "virtual peonage," chained to "worn out soil most did not own, with little hope for an improvement in their lives."[4] These educators proved quite adept at confronting their hostile environs in order to assure the survival of their schools. Edwards built an alliance and close personal relationship with a white planter, but he remained estranged from the majority of whites in his community despite prodding from Tuskegee to "get hold of the white people in your county."[5] He chose, instead, to build his school a mile-and-a-half from the town of Snow Hill as a way to emphasize the separatist and self-determining nature of his endeavor. Edwards used location rather than elocution as a visible symbol of protest against racism.

Holtzclaw proved more adept than his Snow Hill mentor at developing accords with important black and white figures in his community. He did not have a white planter to depend upon. The Utica principal received crucial support from the black clergy as well as from a number of prominent Mississippi whites who joined his board of trustees. Holtzclaw also built his school five miles from local whites and nurtured black self-development through his Community Court of Justice. Again, distance and not rhetoric became part of a black educator's arsenal for survival.

Not far from Utica, the Missouri-born and Iowa-educated Jones skillfully cultivated support from southern whites in order to gain northern contributions. A white contemporary remembered that Jones told him that "he was getting some small donations from friends up North. He said, 'You see, Mr. Webster, . . . they believe that you white people down here are going to help me and not hinder me.' " His most eminent biographer concluded that "Piney Woods could not exist in the midst of the Mississippi community without reflecting . . . the color line and Jim Crow system prevalent in that society."[6] One of the first black students to attend the Piney Woods School also recalled that Jones "seemed like he got along just fine with the white people around here. If he ever had any trouble with any white folks it was off somewhere else. It wasn't here."[7] Like Edwards and Holtzclaw, Jones nurtured his school away from the local white community (three miles, in his case), maintaining needed relationships with whites while developing a separate existence among black people.

Fuller devised his racial strategy in the city, using the *Memphis Commercial Appeal* to publicize his views. He once revealed to a gathering of black Memphis ministers that "I meet . . . white editors especially, and I write editorials for papers. By coming in contact with them I am enabled . . . to reach the white people of the community. I can get into the papers whatever I wish." He also developed a congenial relationship with white editors in order to attract attention to his school: "The white publications have been a silent force helping us. As the readers read in the daily papers, they have talked among themselves, and the boys and girls hear it, and so the knowledge is spread."[8] Fuller received access to the *Commercial Appeal* no doubt because of his public acquiescence to segregation. But, as historian David Tucker has discovered, Fuller also shrewdly used the press to hide the nonindustrial features of his school: "Few local whites . . . were even aware of Howe's academic program since the prudent Reverend Fuller publicized only the school's industrial training. . . . Fuller saw to it that it got wide coverage in the white press, and nothing ever had to be said about the courses in Greek and psychology."[9]

It is difficult to determine whether race relations were positively affected by these educators and their schools. Lynchings continued unabated, and public support for black education declined. Jones probably made the most overt gestures to foster racial harmony. John R. Wesbster, a white supporter, recalled that Jones was "our very best neighbor. He would send his students to help some sick family with their crop, or as a servant in the house if there was a new baby or a death in the family. He would send his choir to sing for aged people who could not go to church."[10] None of these educators could afford the luxury of direct confrontation, and they chose instead to mix concession and conciliation with the weapons of self-reliance and separation. They were modern realists of the first order who were aware of the function of manual training as a basis for compromise. Washington expressed this notion concisely: "Just here is where the great mission of industrial education comes in. It secures the cooperation of the whites, and does the best possible thing for the black man."[11]

The second contextual "R" for these educators was ruralism. Without exception, they recognized the agrarian roots of black people and celebrated the virtues of the country. The schools at Snow Hill, Utica, and the Piney Woods addressed the problems of rural life through extension services like farmers' conferences designed to inform and Black Belt Improvement Societies intended to reform and revitalize community life. Fuller, the city dweller, also indulged in rural rhapsodies, referring to the "fresh, pure air of the farm, where the copious showers of nature fall in lovely smiles upon forest and field . . . [and where] the dangers [are] less."[12] Homage to ruralism was matched only by the belief that the South was the best place for blacks to live. These educators adhered to a "doctrine of permanence" and regarded the South as "the soul of black being [and] the germinative womb out of which the Negro's entire existence and cultural identity inextricably rose and evolved." They fervently opposed black migration, refusing to view the North as a "generous life-giver" or stigmatize the South as the "implacable oppressor" of black people.[13]

The southern roots of three of these educators were therefore strong and deep. (Although Jones was not a southerner by birth, he had left the Midwest at the age of twenty-five, and he returned only periodically to raise funds for his school.) But in the case of Snow Hill Institute, alumni did not accept the message that migration was a mistake. Edwards's students left the Black Belt for northern and southern cities and rejected the notion that they could advance and lift themselves up amidst their rural roots. Although the records are sparse, Snow Hill's failure was probably shared by the other schools in this study.

The schools that these educators built were designed as tools to shape proper behavior. Reformation of character became as compelling a concern as racism and ruralism. Students were expected to obey rules and regulations and follow precise routines that would, according to their principals, build disposition and remove the deficits of unstable homes. Edwards sought "lost boys [and] girls" who could become, under his care, "better men and better women." Holtzclaw reveled in pupils who were "literally transformed in soul and body . . . because of the new atmosphere in which [they have] been permitted to live."[14] Jones likened his students to "human orchards" in need of "spraying," and Fuller claimed that "pluck and energy based upon purity of character" guaranteed success.[15] An emphasis on character development was a logical and significant manifestation of their beliefs.

The lives and experiences of these educators embodied the possibility of self-improvement. Each assumed a responsibility for the uplift of his students and his community. Each believed that education was the pathway for black people to reach their potential and that their schools would provide black students with a chance to be honest, self-respecting, and hardworking members of society. Born after the sorrow of slavery and passed on in expectation by what historian Herbert Gutman has called the "self-activities" of black people to educate themselves after emancipation, Snow Hill, Utica, and Howe institutes and the Piney Woods School represented educational initiatives for problems that needed to be solved, voices that needed to be heard, and responsibilities that needed to be met.[16]

An examination of selected policies, practices, and processes in use at these schools from their founding until 1915 does not reveal any exploitation of the aspirations of black students. These educators did not seek to "educate for servitude" or "school for a new slavery."[17] They were committed to black survival in the rural South and conceived their efforts as opportunities for service. The conditions under which they worked and the difficulties, disappointments, and discouragements that they encountered all reflected the need for patience, dedication, and hard work. But Afro-American educational history is better understood when process and product are analyzed. In the case of these schools, rhetoric and reality were not often congruent. They hovered frequently between the bright lights of triumph and the shadows of defeat. As declarations of possibility, they represented the beginnings of a solution rather than the end of the problem. For Edwards, Holtzclaw, Jones, and Fuller, the realities of black educational leadership always seemed to have been located between struggle and hope.

Notes

Preface

1. Monroe N. Work, *Industrial Work of Tuskegee Graduates and Former Students during the Year 1910* (Tuskegee Institute, Ala., 1911), 47. Replicas of Tuskegee were established or headed by Tuskegee graduates in Alabama, Arkansas, South Carolina, Tennessee, Louisiana, Florida, Mississippi, and Virginia.

2. Raymond Gavins, "Gordon Blaine Hancock: A Black Profile from the New South," *Journal of Negro History* 59 (July 1974): 207.

3. Elizabeth Jacoway, *Yankee Missionaries in the South: The Penn School Experiment* (Baton Rouge, La., 1980), 3–4, 21.

4. Robert G. Sherer, *Subordination or Liberation?: The Development and Conflicting Theories of Black Education in Nineteenth Century Alabama* (University, Ala., 1977), viii.

Chapter One

1. Robert G. Sherer, *Subordination or Liberation?: The Development and Conflicting Theories of Black Education in Nineteenth Century Alabama* (University, Ala., 1977), 78; Joseph F. Citro, "Booker T. Washington's Tuskegee Institute: Black School-Community, 1900–1915" (Ed.D. diss., University of Rochester, 1973), 505.

2. Monroe N. Work, *Industrial Work of Tuskegee Graduates and Former Students during the Year 1910* (Tuskegee Institute, Ala., 1911), 51. Abner B. Jackson also established the Jacksonian Enterprise School at Newville, Alabama, in 1893.

3. Biographical data about Edwards can be found in Clement Richardson, ed., *The National Cyclopedia of the Colored Race* (Montgomery, Ala., 1919), 40–41; and J. H. Moorman and E. C. Barrett, eds., *Leaders of the Colored Race in Alabama* (Mobile, Ala., 1928), 67. For a description of Edwards's student days at Tuskegee, see Booker T. Washington, "Signs of Progress among the Negroes," *Century Magazine* 59 (January 1900): 472–74. Edwards wrote an autobiography, *Twenty-Five Years in the Black Belt* (Boston, 1918), which is a compilation of writings published throughout his career.

4. William J. Edwards, "Some Results of the Snow Hill Normal and Industrial Institute, 1894–1910," Sterling Library, Yale University, New Haven, Conn.

5. William J. Edwards, "Uplifting the Submerged Masses," in *Tuskegee and Its People: Their Ideals and Achievements,* ed. Booker T. Washington (New York, 1905; reprint, New York, 1969), 225; Edwards, *Twenty-Five Years,* 23–24.

6. Louis R. Harlan, *Booker T. Washington: The Wizard of Tuskegee, 1901–1915* (New York, 1983), 170.

7. "Review of the History of the Snow Hill Normal and Industrial Institute," *The Black Belt,* July 1899, Microfilm Records of The Snow Hill Institute, SNI.2, Talladega College Historical Collections, Talladega, Ala. (Hereafter cited as Snow Hill Records or SHR.) Edwards also described his trip in "Uplifting the Submerged Masses," 229–40.

8. The establishment of Tuskegee Institute occurred when black people in Macon County agreed to support a white lawyer for the state senate if he agreed, upon being elected, to work for the creation of a school for the county's black population. Once the school was funded, the board of commissioners asked Samuel Chapman Armstrong, the white founder of Hampton Institute, to suggest a candidate to head the school. Armstrong recommended Booker T. Washington, and his suggestion was accepted with a telegram that read: "Booker T. Washington will suit us. Send him at once." See Basil Mathews, *Booker T. Washington: Educator and Interracial Interpreter* (Cambridge, 1948), 62–63; Louis R. Harlan, *Booker T. Washington: The Making of a Black Leader, 1856–1901* (New York, 1972), 115.

9. "Review of the History of the Snow Hill Institute"; Edwards, "Uplifting the Submerged Masses," 240.

10. Edwards, "Uplifting the Submerged Masses," 241–42; *Tenth Annual Report of the Principal and Treasurer of the Snow Hill Normal and Industrial Institute,* 5 May 1904, SHR, SNI.2.

11. William J. Edwards to Booker T. Washington, 5 September 1894, Booker T. Washington Papers, Manuscripts Division, Library of Congress (hereafter cited as BTW Papers).

12. Harlan, *The Making of a Black Leader,* 122.

13. William J. Edwards to Booker T. Washington, 5 September 1894, BTW Papers.

14. William J. Edwards to Booker T. Washington, 27 November 1896, BTW Papers.

15. *Fifth Annual Report of the Principal* [of Snow Hill Institute], 10 May 1899, SHR, SNI.2. Edwards received his first major donation when Andrew Carnegie gave his school ten thousand dollars in 1906. Snow Hill Institute also received assistance from the Slater Fund, the Rosenwald Fund, and the Southern Education Fund. See Enck, "Black Self-Help."

16. Edwards, *Twenty-Five Years,* 45–47; Henry S. Enck, "Black Self-Help in the Progressive Era: The 'Northern Campaigns' of Smaller Southern Black Industrial Schools, 1900–1915," *Journal of Negro History* 61 (January 1976): 73–87; *The Black Belt* 4 (August 1902): 2, J. G. Phelps Stokes Papers, Box 18, "Misc. Negro Schools" folder, Rare Book and Manuscript Library, Columbia University Library, New York.

17. *Thirty Years of Lynching in the United States, 1889–1918* (New York, 1919), 35,47. The lynchings in Wilcox County occurred in 1904 and 1905.

18. Glen Sisk, "The Educational Awakening in Alabama and its Effect upon the Black Belt, 1900–1917," *Journal of Negro Education* 25 (Spring 1956): 193; U.S. Department of the Interior, Census Office, *Thirteenth Census of the United States, 1910: Population* (Washington, 1913), 2:59.

19. William J. Edwards to Emmett J. Scott, 18 June 1912, BTW Papers.

20. Simpson was born in Belleville, Alabama, in 1842. After the Civil War, he planted cotton and prospered. He died in 1926. See *The Booker T. Washington Papers,* 13 vols., ed. Louis R. Harlan, et al., (Urbana, Ill., 1972–84), 3:530–31.

21. Edwards, *Twenty-Five Years,* 39–56; Washington, "Signs of Progress among the Negroes," 472–78.

22. Booker T. Washington, "A Man About Whom the World Should Know," *The Independent* 58 (May 1905): 1116; William J. Edwards to Booker T. Washington, 5 September 1894, BTW Papers. Simpson served on the Board of Trustees of Tuskegee Institute from 1896 until his death in 1926. His service on the Snow Hill Institute board started in 1898.

23. Washington, "A Man About Whom the World Should Know," 1116; Edwards, *Twenty-Five Years,* 56–57.

24. *Eighteenth Annual Report of the Principal and Treasurer of the Snow Hill Normal and Industrial Institute,* 1911–12, SHR, SNI.2; Sandra Kissick, "The Theme of Exodus Versus Permanence in the South in Negro Autobiographies Published Between 1900 and 1915" (Ph.D. diss., University of Michigan, 1972), 94–95.

25. Booker T. Washington to William J. Edwards, 30 November 1914, BTW Papers; William J. Edwards to Booker T. Washington, 1 December 1914, BTW Papers.

26. William J. Edwards to Booker T. Washington, 5 September 1894, BTW Papers. Typical references to location appear in *Fifth Annual Report of the Principal* [of Snow Hill Institute] and *Tenth Annual Report of the Principal and Treasurer of Snow Hill.*

27. William J. Edwards to "My Dear Friend," 20 July 1910, Snow Hill File, Peabody Education Fund Papers, Special Collection, the Jean and Alexander Heard Library, Vanderbilt University, Nashville,

Tenn. (hereafter referred to as PEFP); William J. Edwards, "An Appeal for the Snow Hill Normal and Industrial Institute," 1911, Snow Hill File, PEFP; William J. Edwards, "Snow Hill Institute, a Light in the Black Belt," 1913, Snow Hill File, PEFP; William Pickens,"The Talladega Letter on Snow Hill," *Alexander's Magazine* 2 (May 1906): 18.

28. In 1890, there were 24,022 blacks and 6,794 whites living in Wilcox County; see U.S. Department of the Interior, Census Office, *Eleventh Census of the United States, 1890: Population* (Washington, 1895), 1:402. The population of Wilcox County in 1910 included 27,062 blacks and 6,208 whites. See *Thirteenth Census of the United States, 1910: Population* 2:34, 58.

29. Edwards, *Twenty-Five Years,* 115-19.

30. William J. Edwards, "Educational and Religious Needs of the Southern Negro" (Address before Lake Placid Club, New York, 1903), SHR, SNI.6; William J. Edwards to "My Dear Friend," 20 July 1910, Snow Hill File, PEFP; "Snow Hill Institute," 1910, SHR, SNI.6.

31. William J. Edwards to Booker T. Washington, 23 February 1909, BTW Papers.

32. "Review of the History of the Snow Hill Institute"; William J. Edwards, "The Signs of the Time," n.d., SHR, SNI.6; Edwards, *Twenty-Five Years,* 62; Edwards, "Uplifting the Submerged Masses," 240.

33. Edwards, *Twenty-Five Years,* 134-35, 141; Edwards, "Educational and Religious Needs."

34. *Fourteenth Annual Catalogue of the Snow Hill Normal and Industrial Institute,* 1907-8, 6, 9, Alabama Department of Archives and History, Montgomery, Ala. (hereafter cited as ADAH); *Seventeenth Annual Catalogue of the Snow Hill Normal and Industrial Institute,* 1911-12, 6, SHR, SNI.3; *Tenth Annual Catalogue of the Snow Hill Normal and Industrial Institute,* 1903-4, 13, ADAH. Capitalization in the original.

35. *Tenth Annual Report of the Principal and Treasurer of Snow Hill; Fourteenth Annual Catalogue of Snow Hill,* 16; *Eighth Annual Catalogue of the Snow Hill Normal and Industrial Institute,* 1901-2, 2, ADAH; William J. Edwards, "Some Results of the Snow Hill Normal and Industrial Institute, 1894-1910," Snow Hill File, PEFP.

36. See Joseph Davis, "A Historical Study of Snow Hill Normal and Industrial Institute and its Contribution to the Educational Program of the State of Alabama" (M.Ed. thesis, Alabama State College, 1954), 23, for mention of *Bible* course; Edwards, "Educational and Religious Needs"; Edwards, "Uplifting the Submerged Masses," 233-34, 236.

37. *Tenth Annual Report of the Principal and Treasurer of Snow Hill;* "An Appeal for the Snow Hill Normal and Industrial Institute, Snow Hill, Ala.," 1911, Snow Hill File, PEFP.

38. *The Black Belt* 4:3; "Speech of William J. Edwards," *Alexan-*

der's Magazine 2 (May 1906): 64–65; *Eleventh Annual Report of the Principal and Treasurer of the Snow Hill Normal and Industrial Institute,* 1905, SHR, SNI.2. The black population in Wilcox County declined from 28,652 in 1900 to 27,602 in 1910.

39. Kissick, "The Theme of Exodus Versus Permanence," 180; William J. Edwards, "Sowing and Reaping," 23 January 1921, SHR, SNI.6.

40. *The Black Belt* 4:3.

41. Edwards, "Uplifting the Submerged Masses," 245–50; Edwards, *Twenty-Five Years,* 42.

42. Edwards, *Twenty-Five Years,* 249–50.

43. *Fifth Annual Catalogue of the Snow Hill Normal and Industrial Institute,* 1898–99, 12–19, ADAH. Snow Hill Institute first reported its enrollment to the United States Bureau of Education in 1903. See U.S. Bureau of Education, *Report of the Commissioner of Education for the Year 1902–1903* (Washington, 1903), 2:2268–69; *1903–1904* 2:1718–19; *1904–1905* 1:806–7; *1905–1906* 1:688–89; *1906–1907* 2:1036–1037; *1907–1908* 2:832–33; *1908–1909* 2:675–76; *1909–1910* 2:593–94; *1910–1911* 2:849–50; *1911–1912* 2:737–38; *1912–1913* 2:612–13; *1913–1914* 2:769–70; *1914–1915* 2:833–34. Female enrollment comprised as much as 56 percent in 1907 and as little as 53 percent in 1913.

44. U.S. Bureau of Education, *Report of the Commissioner of Education, from 1902–1903 to 1914–1915.* Class lists by grade appear in the fifth (1898–99), eighth (1901–2), fourteenth (1907–8) and twenty-third (1916–17) annual catalogues of the school.

45. Edwards, "Uplifting the Submerged Masses," 242–43; U.S. Bureau of Labor, *Twenty-Fifth Annual Report of the Commissioner of Labor, 1910,* 328.

46. *Twenty-Seventh Annual Catalogue of Snow Hill Normal and Industrial Institute,* 1920–21, SHR, SNI.3. Snow Hill listed 141 normal school graduates from 1899 to 1915, but only 89 had their employment status listed. Of this number, 10 worked at Snow Hill Institute, 15 taught in Alabama, and 9 were employed in Florida, Mississippi, and North Carolina. Five of these graduates taught at Laurinburg Normal and Industrial Institute in North Carolina, and 2 were employed at Utica Industrial Institute in Mississippi.

47. Ibid. Of the industrial education graduates who migrated north, four lived in Chicago, two in Cleveland, one in Pittsburgh, one in Detroit, and one in Auburdale, Massachusetts. The employment status of alumni with trade certificates was not designated.

48. *Fifth Annual Report of the Principal; Eighth Annual Catalogue of Snow Hill,* 5; *Fourteenth Annual Catalogue of Snow Hill,* 14; *Seventeenth Annual Catalogue of Snow Hill,* 15, 11.

49. Snow Hill Visitation Committee to Booker T. Washington, 15 April 1910, BTW Papers.

50. *Fourteenth Annual Catalogue of Snow Hill,* 10; William J.

Edwards to Booker T. Washington, 21 September 1899, BTW Papers; Edwards, *Twenty-Five Years*, 141–42.

51. Edwards, "The Signs of the Time"; *Fifth Annual Catalogue of Snow Hill*, 11; *Eighth Annual Catalogue of Snow Hill*, 11, 12.

52. *Tenth Annual Report of the Principal and Treasurer of Snow Hill; Seventeenth Annual Catalogue of Snow Hill*, 22; *Eighteenth Annual Report of the Principal and Treasurer of Snow Hill*.

53. Snow Hill Visitation Committee to Booker T. Washington, 15 April 1910, BTW Papers.

54. Ibid.

55. Robert E. Park to Booker T. Washington, 6 April 1913, BTW Papers; Booker T. Washington to William J. Edwards, 15 August 1913, BTW Papers; William J. Edwards to Booker T. Washington, 7 August 1913, BTW Papers.

56. Robert E. Park to Booker T. Washington, 29 May 1913, *The BTW Papers* 12:192–93.

57. Edwards, "Uplifting the Submerged Masses," 252.

Chapter Two

1. Holtzclaw provided details about his birth in his autobiography, *The Black Man's Burden* (New York, 1915), 13. For a brief sketch of Holtzclaw's life from 1870 to 1918, see Clement Richardson, ed., *The National Cyclopedia of the Colored Race* (Montgomery, Ala., 1919), 450. R. Fulton Holtzclaw has written a biography of his father that should be consulted. See *William Henry Holtzclaw: Scholar in Ebony* (Cleveland, 1977).

2. William H. Holtzclaw, "A Negro's Life Story," *World's Work* 12 (September 1906): 7990.

3. Ibid., 7991.

4. Ibid.

5. Holtzclaw, *The Black Man's Burden*, 52.

6. Ibid., 61.

7. Ibid., 62. The class motto is mentioned in Booker T. Washington, ed., *Tuskegee and Its People: Their Ideals and Achievements* (New York, 1905; reprint, New York, 1969), 263.

8. Holtzclaw, "A Negro's Life Story," 7992.

9. Holtzclaw, *The Black Man's Burden*, 64.

10. Ibid., 65–66.

11. William H. Holtzclaw, "A School Principal's Story," in Washington, *Tuskegee and Its People*, 132.

12. Holtzclaw, *The Black Man's Burden*, 111.

13. William H. Holtzclaw to Booker T. Washington, 19 July 1902, Booker T. Washington Papers, Manuscripts Division, Library of Congress (hereafter cited as BTW Papers).

14. Holtzclaw, *The Black Man's Burden,* 70, 75–76. Mound Bayou is an all-black town founded in 1887. Bolivar County, where Mound Bayou is located, had 31,197 blacks (88 percent) and 4,197 whites in 1900. See *The Booker T. Washington Papers,* 13 vols., ed. Louis R. Harlan, et al. (Urbana, Ill., 1972–84), 3:84–85; U.S. Department of the Interior, Census Office, *Twelfth Census of the United States, 1900: Population* (Washington, 1902) 1:545.

15. Holtzclaw, *The Black Man's Burden,* 75, 182.

16. Ibid., 82–86.

17. Ibid., 82–83.

18. Ibid., 86; Thomas Jesse Jones, ed., *Negro Education: A Study of the Private and Higher Schools for Colored People in the United States,* 2 vols. (Washington, D.C., 1917), 2:351–58.

19. *Southern Notes,* May 1911; *Fifth Annual Financial Statement of the Principal and Treasurer of the Utica, Mississippi, Normal and Industrial Institute, for the Year Ending May 4, 1908,* 1. *Southern Notes* was the newsletter of Utica Institute. Scattered issues are in the Sterling Library, Yale University.

20. Emma C. Penney, "A Light in the Black Belt of Mississippi," *Alexander's Magazine* 5 (November 1907): 25. Penney was a teacher at Utica Institute. Fraudulent financial appeals by industrial school fund-raisers was not uncommon and cast a "damaging stigma on the efforts of legitimate representatives of black industrial schools." See Henry Snyder Enck, "The Burden Borne: Northern White Philanthropy and Southern Black Industrial Education, 1900–1915" (Ph.D., diss., University of Cincinnati, 1970), 408–9.

21. Holtzclaw, *The Black Man's Burden,* 89–90.

22. *Charter of Incorporation of The Utica Normal and Industrial Institute,* 13 January 1903, Office of Secretary of State, Jackson, Miss.

23. Holtzclaw, *The Black Man's Burden,* 95–97.

24. Ibid., 100. The other two trustees were white northerners, one of whom was Rev. R. C. Bedford, Booker T. Washington's confidant. See *Charter of Incorporation of the Utica Normal and Industrial Institute.*

25. Holtzclaw, *The Black Man's Burden,* 100, 102.

26. *Southern Notes,* May 1911; Holtzclaw, *The Black Man's Burden,* 102.

27. Holtzclaw, *The Black Man's Burden,* 122.

28. *Twelfth Census of the United States* 1:545; U.S. Department of the Interior, Census Office, *Thirteenth Census of the United States, 1910: Population,* (Washington, 1913), 2:1048.

29. *Southern Notes,* September 1906, May 1911, and January 1915.

30. C. Vann Woodward, *Origins of the New South, 1877–1913* (Baton Rouge, La., 1951), 121; Stuart Grayson Noble, *Forty Years of the Public Schools in Mississippi* (New York, 1918), 53–54.

31. Henry Allen Bullock, *A History of Negro Education in the South from 1619 to the Present* (Cambridge, 1967), 180–81; *Thirteenth Census of the United States* 2:1048. The Census Office defined illiteracy as the inability to read and write.

32. Eugene E. White, "Anti-Racial Agitation in Politics: James Kimble Vardaman in the Mississippi Gubernatorial Campaign of 1903," *Journal of Mississippi History* 7 (April 1945): 91–110; Vardaman quoted in Noble, *Forty Years,* 96.

33. Albert D. Kirwan, *Revolt of the Rednecks: Mississippi Politics, 1876–1925* (Lexington, Ky., 1951), 147–48.

34. Holtzclaw, *The Black Man's Burden,* 98–99.

35. *Southern Notes,* September 1906.

36. Holtzclaw, *The Black Man's Burden,* 124.

37. Emmett J. Scott to Julius Rosenwald, 29 April 1912, BTW Papers.

38. Holtzclaw, *The Black Man's Burden,* 145.

39. Ibid., 167–70.

40. *Thirty Years of Lynching in the United States, 1889–1918* (New York, 1919), 35, 77–78. The lynchings in Hinds County occurred in 1899 (two), 1901 (one), and 1906 (one). None occurred in Utica.

41. Holtzclaw, *The Black Man's Burden,* 106–210; *Jackson Daily News,* 12 February 1911. Noel was governor of Mississippi from 1908 to 1912. No correspondence between Holtzclaw and Noel has been discovered to corroborate Holtzclaw's claim that he protested lynchings.

42. This postcard was sent to Booker T. Washington.

43. Holtzclaw, *The Black Man's Burden,* 106.

44. Ibid., 102; Penney, "A Light in the Black Belt," 27. Utica Institute did not begin to report enrollment data to the U.S. Bureau of Education until 1908–9. A study of these figures reveals that the peak enrollment for the period 1908–15 was reached in 1911–12, when 425 students were reported. See U.S. Bureau of Education, *Report of the Commissioner of Education,* 1908–15 (Washington, 1915).

45. *Seventh Annual Financial Statement of the Principal and Treasurer of the Utica, Mississippi, Normal and Industrial Institute, for the Year Ending June 1, 1910,* 3; Holtzclaw, *The Black Man's Burden,* 105–6.

46. Holtzclaw, *The Black Man's Burden,* 221–22. The daily schedule at Utica practically duplicated the routine that Holtzclaw knew as a student at Tuskegee. See Booker T. Washington, *Up from Slavery* (New York, 1901; reprint, Garden City, N.Y., 1929), 314.

47. Holtzclaw, *The Black Man's Burden,* 227, 116; *Fifth Annual Statement of the Principal and Treasurer of the Utica Normal and Industrial Institute, for the Year Ending May 2, 1907,* 1.

48. Monroe Nathan Work, *Industrial Work of Tuskegee Graduates and Former Students during the Year 1910* (Tuskegee Institute,

Ala., 1911), 57; *Annual Report Edition of the Principal and Treasurer, Utica Institute, 1914,* 3.

49. *Sixth Annual Financial Statement of the Principal and Treasurer of the Utica, Mississippi, Normal and Industrial Institute, for the Year Ending May 4, 1909,* 3. Holtzclaw claimed in his autobiography that by 1915 "about six hundred young men and women have been educated and sent into various parts of the state." See *The Black Man's Burden,* 222.

50. *Southern Notes,* May 1911.

51. Ibid. One Utica Institute normal school graduate established the Spring Hill Normal and Industrial School in Florence, Mississippi, in 1904. Another founded the Mississippi High School at Crystal Springs in Copiah County in 1907. See Work, *Industrial Work of Tuskegee Graduates,* 57. The activities of several graduates are highlighted in *Southern Notes,* September 1906, May 1911, and January 1915.

52. *Report of the Principal and Treasurer of the Utica Normal and Industril [sic] Institute, for the Year Ending June 1, 1912,* 7.

53. *Southern Notes,* September 1906; *Report of Utica Institute for 1912,* 183, 120.

54. Jones, *Negro Education* 2:348–49.

55. Holtzclaw, *The Black Man's Burden,* 119–20.

56. Ibid., 211.

57. *Report of the Principal and Treasurer of the Utica Normal and Industrial Institute, for the Year Ending June 1, 1913,* 3.

58. Holtzclaw, "A School Principal's Story," 138–39; Penney, "A Light in the Black Belt," 25.

59. H. D. Slatter, "Noble Work in the Black Belt," *Alexander's Magazine* 1(May 1905): 20; work, *Industrial Work of Tuskegee Graduates,* 56. Holtzclaw's son noted that his mother became the postmistress when a U.S. Post Office was established on the Utica campus in 1913. See R. F. Holtzclaw, *William Henry Holtzclaw,* 224.

60. Lizette Strong to George Washington Carver, 23 January 1905, George Washington Carver Papers (microfilm edition, reel 3, series II), Tuskegee Institute Archives, Tuskegee University, Ala.

61. See letterhead on stationery used by Laurence C. Jones (director of the Academic Department) to the director of the Roger's Fund, 29 March 1909, BTW Papers; Holtzclaw, *The Black Man's Burden,* 164.

62. Slatter, "Noble Work," 20. Tougaloo College was founded by the American Missionary Association in 1869. Laurence C. Jones was the faculty member who graduated from the University of Iowa.

63. William Pickens, "Utica," *The Independent* 72 (February 1912): 405–7.

64. Holtzclaw, *The Black Man's Burden,* 197. I have found only one reference to the salaries of Utica faculty, and that indicated that

teachers were paid ten dollars for a two-month summer session. See *Southern Notes,* September 1906. Holtzclaw's son maintained that his father's salary was set in 1903 at $2,500 and that this amount remained constant "through recession, depression, and inflation for forty years." See R. F. Holtzclaw, *William Henry Holtzclaw,* 85–86.

65. Jones, *Negro Education* 2:349.

66. Work, *Industrial Work of Tuskegee Graduates,* 56; Holtzclaw, *The Black Man's Burden,* 129–30; *Fifth Annual Statement of Utica Institute* (1907), 5.

67. *Jackson Daily News,* 12 February 1909. Holtzclaw provides examples of the testimonies of black farmers at the farmers' conferences in *The Black Man's Burden,* 146–51.

68. Holtzclaw, *The Black Man's Burden,* 134–35.

69. *Report of the Principal of Utica Institute* (1913), 9–10; Holtzclaw, *The Black Man's Burden,* 136–39.

70. Holtzclaw, *The Black Man's Burden,* 139–41.

71. Sandra Kissick, "The Theme of Exodus Versus Permanence in the South in Negro Autobiographies Published Between 1900 and 1915" (Ph.D. diss., University of Michigan, 1972), 86–87.

72. Enck, "The Burden Borne," 443; Holtzclaw, *The Black Man's Burden,* 212.

73. Holtzclaw, *The Black Man's Burden,* 124–25.

74. Ibid., 123, 232.

Chapter Three

1. Louis R. Harlan, *Booker T. Washington: The Wizard of Tuskegee, 1901–1915* (New York, 1983), 170; *Southern Letter,* March 1893, cited in Joseph F. Citro, "Booker T. Washington's Tuskegee Institute: Black School-Community, 1900–1915" (Ed.D. diss., University of Rochester, 1973), 469.

2. Louis R. Harlan, *Booker T. Washington: The Making of a Black Leader, 1856–1901* (New York, 1972), 254, 271; Harlan also discusses the Tuskegee Machine in *The Wizard of Tuskegee,* 106.

3. Harlan, *The Making of a Black Leader,* 271.

4. Booker T. Washington, *Working with the Hands* (New York, 1904), 219, 222–25.

5. Booker T. Washington, ed., *Tuskegee and Its People: Their Ideals and Achievements* (New York, 1905; reprint, New York, 1969), 13, 224–52, 111–40.

6. Monroe N. Work, *Industrial Work of Tuskegee Graduates and Former Students during the Year 1910* (Tuskegee Institute, Ala., 1911), 53–57.

7. Booker T. Washington, "Signs of Progress among the Negroes," *Century Magazine* 59 (January 1900): 472–74. *Century Maga-*

zine had a circulation of 125,000 in 1900. See Frank Luther Mott, *A History of American Magazines,* 5 vols. (Cambridge, 1938–68), 3: 3, 475.

8. Booker T. Washington, "A Cheerful Journey through Mississippi," *World's Work* 17 (February 1909): 11278–82. The circulation of *World's Work* in 1909 was 100,000. See Mott, *A History of American Magazines* 4: 773, 780, 783.

9. Citro, "Booker T. Washington's Tuskegee Institute," 498, 509.

10. Henry Snyder Enck, "The Burden Borne: Northern White Philanthropy and Southern Black Industrial Education, 1900–1915" (Ph.D. diss., University of Cincinnati, 1970), 78.

11. William J. Edwards to Booker T. Washington, 16 November 1899 and 22 November 1899, Booker T. Washington Papers, Manuscripts Division, Library of Congress (hereafter cited as BTW Papers).

12. William J. Edwards to Booker T. Washington, 3 November 1902, BTW Papers.

13. Booker T. Washington to Emmett J. Scott, 31 January 1907, *The Booker T. Washington Papers,* 13 vols., ed. Louis B. Harlan, et al., (Urbana, Ill., 1972–84), 9:205–6. William J. Edwards to Booker T. Washington, 29 May 1902 and 28 February 1905, BTW Papers.

14. Booker T. Washington to Jacob Henry Schiff, 18 September 1909, *The Booker T. Washington Papers* 10:175–76; William J. Edwards to Booker T. Washington, 17 September 1915, BTW Papers; Booker T. Washington to William J. Edwards, 16 July 1914, BTW Papers; William J. Edwards to Booker T. Washington, 31 May 1915, BTW Papers. Julius Rosenwald was president of Sears, Roebuck and Co. and a member of the board of trustees of Tuskegee Institute. John F. Slater, a textile industrialist from Connecticut, established a fund in 1882 to assist public and private schools in the South.

15. William J. Edwards to Booker T. Washington, 3 November 1911, BTW Papers; Booker T. Washington to William J. Edwards, 5 and 11 November 1911, BTW Papers; William J. Edwards to Booker T. Washington, 9 November 1911, BTW Papers.

16. Henry S. Enck, "Black Self-Help in the Progressive Era: The 'Northern Campaigns' of Smaller Southern Black Industrial Schools, 1900–1915," *Journal of Negro History* 61 (January 1976): 79. Holtzclaw's dependency on Washington can be followed in the following correspondence: William H. Holtzclaw to Booker T. Washington, 2 June 1908, BTW Papers; William H. Holtzclaw to "My Dear Friend," 3 June 1908, BTW Papers; Booker T. Washington to William H. Holtzclaw, 8 June 1908, BTW Papers; William H. Holtzclaw to Booker T. Washington, 10 June 1908, BTW Papers.

17. William H. Holtzclaw to Booker T. Washington, 14 February 1909, BTW Papers; Booker T. Washington to William H. Holtzclaw, 20 February 1909, BTW Papers.

18. Booker T. Washington to Jacob Henry Schiff, 18 September 1909, and Booker T. Washington to Sarah Newlin, 4 December 1909,

The Booker T. Washington Papers 10: 175–76, 241.

19. William H. Holtzclaw to Booker T. Washington, 10 June 1910, BTW Papers; Booker T. Washington to William H. Holtzclaw, 16 June 1910, BTW Papers; Booker T. Washington to E. H. Paul, 28 July 1910, *The Booker T. Washington Papers* 10: 357.

20. William H. Holtzclaw to Booker T. Washington, 5 August 1910, BTW Papers; Booker T. Washington to William H. Holtzclaw, 8 August 1910, BTW Papers.

21. William H. Holtzclaw to Booker T. Washington, 22 February 1915 and 1 March 1915, BTW Papers; Booker T. Washington to William H. Holtzclaw, 27 February 1915, BTW Papers. The General Education Board was established by John D. Rockefeller in 1902.

22. Enck, "Black Self-Help," 79–80.

23. Booker T. Washington to William J. Edwards, 18 May 1908, BTW Papers; William J. Edwards to Booker T. Washington, 20 May 1908, BTW Papers.

24. Booker T. Washington to William J. Edwards, 29 December 1910, BTW Papers.

25. Booker T. Washington to William J. Edwards, 18 February 1915, 18 June 1915, and 6 October 1915, BTW Papers.

26. Between 1901 and 1915 Washington attracted to the Tuskegee Institute Board of Trustees such men as New York investment banker Jacob Henry Schiff, President of Sears, Roebuck and Co. Julius Rosenwald, former President Theodore Roosevelt, and President of the Long Island Railroad William F. Baldwin, Jr. Edwards was never able to attract such influential persons, nor could he attract a geographically diverse trustee board. Eight of the thirteen members of Snow Hill's board in 1899 were from Alabama, and by 1915 three of six board members lived in Alabama. See William J. Edwards to Booker T. Washington, 21 September 1899 and 15 June 1915, BTW Papers.

27. Booker T. Washington to William J. Edwards, 17 February 1909, BTW Papers; William J. Edwards to Booker T. Washington, 23 February 1909, BTW Papers.

28. Booker T. Washington to William J. Edwards, 26 June 1910, BTW Papers.

29. William J. Edwards to Booker T. Washington, 8 July 1910, BTW Papers; Booker T. Washington to William J. Edwards, 17 July 1910, BTW Papers.

30. William H. Holtzclaw to Booker T. Washington, 19 June 1908, BTW Papers; Booker T. Washington to William H. Holtzclaw, 27 February 1915, BTW Papers.

31. William H. Holtzclaw to Booker T. Washington, 23 April 1915, BTW Papers.

32. Harlan, *The Making of a Black Leader*, 260–61; Harlan, *The Wizard of Tuskegee*, xii.

33. Emmett J. Scott to Julius Rosenwald, 29 April 1912, BTW

Papers; William H. Holtzclaw to Emmett J. Scott, 2 May 1912, BTW Papers.

34. Julius Rosenwald to William H. Holtzclaw, 2 May 1912, BTW Papers; William H. Holtzclaw to Emmett J. Scott, 6 May 1912.

35. Emmett J. Scott to William H. Holtzclaw, 2 May 1915 and 6 May 1915, BTW Papers. The Phelps Stokes Fund was established in 1911 in accordance with the will of Carolina Phelps Stokes, heiress to a real estate fortune in New York City. This fund had a special interest in black education in the rural South.

36. William J. Edwards to Booker T. Washington, 17 January 1909, BTW Papers; Booker T. Washington to William J. Edwards, 25 January 1909, BTW Papers.

37. William J. Edwards to Booker T. Washington, 2 April 1912, BTW Papers; Booker T. Washington to William J. Edwards, 27 June 1912, BTW Papers.

38. William J. Edwards to Booker T. Washington, 22 September 1913 and 15 January 1915, BTW Papers; Booker T. Washington to William J. Edwards, 18 January 1915 and 22 January 1915, BTW Papers.

39. William H. Holtzclaw to Booker T. Washington, 14 February 1913, BTW Papers; Booker T. Washington to William H. Holtzclaw, 19 February 1913, BTW Papers; *Report of the Principal and Treasurer of the Utica Normal and Industril [sic] Institute, for the Year Ending June 1, 1912,* 3,

40. See Chapter One, 16–19.

41. Snow Hill Visitation Committee to Booker T. Washington, 15 April 1910, BTW Papers.

42. William J. Edwards to Booker T. Washington, 6 May 1910, BTW Papers.

43. Ibid.

44. Citro, "Booker T. Washington's Tuskegee Institute," 352.

45. William J. Edwards to Booker T. Washington, 2 April 1912, BTW Papers.

46. William J. Edwards to Booker T. Washington, 7 August 1913, BTW Papers.

47. Booker T. Washington to William J. Edwards, 15 August 1913, BTW papers.

48. Ibid.

49. See ANISS letterhead on stationery used by Leslie Pinckney Hill to Oscar Garrison Villard, 2 November 1917, Oscar Garrison Villard Papers, Folder 1323, Houghton Library, Harvard University, Cambridge, Mass.

50. Enck, "Black Self-Help," 86.

51. Charles Flint Kellogg, *NAACP* (Baltimore, 1967), 86.

52. Booker T. Washington to William J. Edwards, 17 May 1915, BTW Papers.

53. William J. Edwards to Booker T. Washington, 24 May 1915, BTW Papers.

54. Emmett J. Scott to William H. Holtzclaw, 26 February 1913, BTW Papers.

55. William H. Holtzclaw to Emmett J. Scott, 3 March 1913, BTW Papers; *The Booker T. Washington Papers* 12: 128.

56. William H. Holtzclaw to Emmett J. Scott, 25 April 1913, BTW Papers.

57. Booker T. Washington to William H. Holtzclaw, 3 May 1913, BTW Papers.

58. William H. Holtzclaw to Emmett J. Scott, 25 May 1913, BTW Papers.

59. William H. Holtzclaw to Emmett J. Scott, 26 November 1913, BTW Papers. Leslie Pinckney Hill was a black graduate of Harvard University who taught at Tuskegee Institute from 1904 to 1907. Hill was fired by Washington because of alleged incompetence. See *The Booker T. Washington Papers* 6: 410; and Citro, "Booker T. Washington's Tuskegee," 170–75.

60. Emmett J. Scott to William H. Holtzclaw, 2 December 1913, BTW Papers.

61. William H. Holtzclaw to Emmett J. Scott, 5 December 1913, BTW Papers.

62. William H. Holtzclaw to Emmett J. Scott, 31 March 1914, BTW Papers.

63. Booker T. Washington to William H. Holtzclaw, 11 May 1915, BTW Papers; William H. Holtzclaw to Booker T. Washington, 13 May 1915, BTW Papers.

64. Enck, "Black Self-Help," 86.

65. William H. Holtzclaw to Booker T. Washington, 24 May 1915, BTW Papers; Booker T. Washington to William H. Holtzclaw, 29 May 1915, BTW Papers.

66. William J. Edwards to Booker T. Washington, 2 April 1912, BTW Papers.

67. Harlan, *The Wizard of Tuskegee,* viii.

68. Washington, *Tuskegee and Its People,* 5.

69. Harlan, *The Wizard of Tuskegee,* 170.

Chapter Four

1. Leslie Harper Purcell, *Miracle in Mississippi: Laurence C. Jones of Piney Woods* (New York, 1956), 1.

2. George A. Sewell, *Mississippi Black History Makers* (Jackson, Miss., 1977), 166–67. The Manual Labor Institute provided training primarily related to agriculture; it had closed by 1856. See Reginald R.

Larrie, *Makin' Free: African-Americans in the Northwest Territory* (Detroit, 1981), 52, 57.

3. Lorenzo J. Greene et al., *Missouri's Black Heritage* (St. Louis, 1980), 95; Laurence C. Jones, *Up through Difficulties* (n.p., 1913), 11–12.

4. Nellie Bass, interview by Alferdteen Harrison, 24 February 1974, OHO1.3b, transcript, Oral History Study of Black Eduational Institutions in Mississippi, Jackson State University Oral History Program, Jackson, Miss. (herefafter cited as OHS with the appropriate interviewee and transcript).

5. Jones, *Up through Difficulties*, 5–6, 13; *Marshalltown Times-Republican*, 29 May 1903.

6. Laurence C. Jones Alumni Vertical Information Folder, University of Iowa Archives, Iowa City, Iowa; Laurence C. Jones, *Piney Woods and Its Story* (New York, 1933), 47; Laurence C. Jones to Thomas H. Macbride, 21 November 1933, Thomas H. Macbride Papers, Folder 2, Box 8, University of Iowa Archives, Iowa City, Iowa. Macbride was President of the University of Iowa from 1914 to 1916 and head of the Botany Department from 1884 to 1914.

7. Jones, *Up through Difficulties*, 16; Jones, *Piney Woods*, 52; Laurence C. Jones to William G. McChesney, 4 September 1903, Laurence C. Jones Alumni Information Vertical Folder; *Des Moines Register and Leader*, 18 June 1911, Magazine section, p. 1.

8. Jones, *Up through Difficulties*, 16–17; Jones, *Piney Woods*, 52–53. Harrison claims that Holtzclaw offered Jones a position at Utica Institute during a visit to Iowa. See Alferdteen Harrison, *Piney Woods School: An Oral History* (Jackson, Miss., 1982), 26.

9. Jones related this account to the *Des Moines Register and Leader*, 18 June 1911. Similar acounts are found in Jones, *Up through Difficulties*, 17–18, and Jones, *Piney Woods*, 54.

10. Jones, *Piney Woods*, 64–66; Harrison, *Piney Woods School*, 29.

11. Jones, *Up through Difficulties*, 25–26; Jones, *Piney Woods*, 61, 67; Harrison, *Piney Woods School*, 30–31.

12. Jones, *Up through Difficulties*, 26; Leola Hughes, interview by Alferdteen Harrison, 5 September 1978, OHO1.4b, transcript, OHS.

13. Jones, *Up through Difficulties*, 28–29; Jones, *Piney Woods*, 68–71.

14. Jones, *Up through Difficulties*, 29; Hughes, interview by Harrison, 5 September 1978.

15. Jones, *Piney Woods*, 71–72; Harrison, *Piney Woods School*, 34–35.

16. *The Pine Torch* 2 (February 1912): 4.

17. U.S. Department of the Interior, Census Office, *Thirteenth*

Census of the United States, 1910: Population (Washington, 1913), 2:
1048, 1056. There were 14,249 blacks in Rankin County out of a total
population of 23,944.

18. Richard A. McLemore, *A History of Mississippi,* 2 vols. (Hattiesburg, Miss., 1973), 2:354.

19. G. S. Dickerman, "From Iowa to Mississippi," *The Crisis* 6
(July 1913): 137.

20. *Thirteenth Census of the United States* 2:1057. In 1910, 35.6
percent of the entire black population of Mississippi was illiterate,
compared with 5.2 percent of the white population.

21. *Thirty Years of Lynching in the United States, 1889–1918*
(New York, 1919), 35, 79–80.

22. Jones, *Up through Difficulties,* 53.

23. Beth Day, *The Little Professor of Piney Woods: The Story of
Laurence Jones* (New York, 1955), 15.

24. *The Pine Torch* 1 (July 1911): 2–3.

25. John R. Webster, *A Brief Historical Sketch of the Early Days
of the Piney Woods School* (Piney Woods, Miss., n.d.), 20, 22. Webster
owned a sawmill in Braxton and was an early patron of Laurence
Jones. He donated lumber for the school's first building. For a view
from an Iowa visitor, see Dickerman, "From Iowa to Mississippi," 138.

26. Jones, *Up through Difficulties,* 56, 74–75; *Jackson Daily
News,* 8 April 1912.

27. Webster, *A Brief Historical Sketch,* 7.

28. *The Pine Torch* 1 (July 1911): 4; Hughes, interview by Harrison, 5 September 1978.

29. *The Pine Torch* 1 (July 1911): 3; *Des Moines Register and
Leader,* 18 June 1911; *The Pine Torch* 5 (November/December 1914):
2; U.S. Bureau of Education, *Report of the Commissioner of Education for the Year 1915–1916* (Washington, 1916), 2:595.

30. Eva Weathersby, interview by Alferdteen Harrison, 27 June
1973, OHO1b.11, transcript, OHS.

31. Jones, *Up through Difficulties,* 63.

32. *The Pine Torch* 3 (February 1913): 3; 3 (January 1913): 4; 4
(November 1913): 1.

33. Jones, *Up through Difficulties,* 67; *The Pine Torch* 4 (November 1913): 1.

34. *The Pine Torch* 3 (January 1913): 3; Jones, *Up through Difficulties,* 42.

35. *The Pine Torch* 3 (February 1913): 3.

36. *The Pine Torch* 5 (November/December 1924): 2; Jones, *Up
through Difficulties,* 79.

37. *The Pine Torch* 3 (August 1913): 3; 3 (September 1913): 1; 5
(May 1914): 1.

38. *The Pine Torch* 4 (October 1913): 3; 5 (November/December
1914): 2–3.

39. Webster, *A Brief Historical Sketch,* 7; Jones, *Up through Difficulties,* 43–44; *Charter of Incorporation of the Piney Woods Country Life School,* 17 May 1913, Office of Secretary of State, Jackson, Miss.

40. *Jackson Daily News,* 20 May 1913; Jones, *Up through Difficulties,* 21–22.

41. Jones, *Up through Difficulties,* 22.

42. Ibid., 26–29.

43. Ibid., 41, 73–74; Harrison, *Piney Woods School,* 55–64.

44. Jones, *Up through Difficulties,* 42–43. The Piney Woods staff was all black from 1909 to 1915; the school had its first white teacher in 1917 when Nellie Brooks from Davenport, Iowa, came to teach for two years. See Harrison, *Piney Woods School,* 93.

45. This designation was always mentioned in the school newsletter during the years 1911–14.

46. Harrison, *Piney Woods School,* 42–44. For descriptions of how Jones's school worked with local farmers, see *The Pine Torch* 2 (February 1912): 4; 4 (April 1912): 2; 2 (September 1912): 1; 2 (May 1912): 1.

47. Jones, *Up through Difficulties,* 69–70.

48. Henry S. Enck, "Black Self-Help in the Progressive Era: The 'Northern Campaigns' of Smaller Southern Black Industrial Schools, 1900–1915," *Journal of Negro History* 61 (January 1976): 73–87; Jones, *Up through Difficulties,* 33; Jones, *Piney Woods,* 75–76; Webster, *A Brief Historical Sketch,* 10–13. Jones was very dependent upon financial donations to operate his school. For example, donations of money comprised 84 percent of his school's total income in 1915. He received in that year only $468 from the counties of Rankin and Simpson. See Thomas Jesse Jones, ed., *Negro Education: A Study of the Private and Higher Schools for Colored People in the United States,* 2 vols. (Washington, D.C., 1917), 2:368.

49. Jones, *Piney Woods,* 79.

50. *Des Moines Iowa State Bystander,* 9 June 1911; Jones, *Up through Difficulties,* 40–41.

51. *The Pine Torch* 5 (May 1911): 1; 5 (August 1914): 1.

52. Jones, *Up through Difficulties,* 57–61.

53. A visitor to the Piney Woods School in 1913 described *The Pine Torch* as "an odd little sheet, printed from type of many sorts and sizes, but alive in very line with the spirit of the man who gets it up, who is author, editor, compositor, printer and publisher, all in one." See Dickerman, "From Iowa to Mississippi," 139–40. *The Pine Torch* cost fifty cents per year during the period 1911–14.

54. *The Pine Torch* 2 (February 1913): 2; 2 (April 1912): 2; 3 (January 1913): 1.

55. *The Pine Torch* 2 (February 1912): 2; 2 (March 1912): 2; 2 (May 1912): 2; 2 (November 1912): 2; 3 (January 1913): 4; 3 (August 1913): 3; 3 (October 1913): 4.

56. The Piney Woods School would eventually receive support
from the Rosenwald and the Slater funds in the 1920s. See Harrison,
Piney Woods School, 67, 96–97.

57. Jones, *Up through Difficulties,* 57. The northeastern orienta-
tion of Tuskegee-affiliated educators is documented in Henry Snyder
Enck, "The Burden Borne: Northern White Philanthropy and Southern
Black Industrial Education, 1900–1915" (Ph.D. diss., University of
Cincinnati, 1970), 461–514; and Enck, "Black Self-Help," 73–87.

58. Jones, *Up through Difficulties,* 77; *The Pine Torch* 5 (Novem-
ber/December 1914): 1–2.

59. *The Pine Torch* 5 (November/December 1914): 3.

60. This motto appeared in each issue of *The Pine Torch.*

Chapter Five

1. Thomas O. Fuller, *Twenty Years in Public Life, 1890–1910*
(Nashville, 1910), 11. A very thorough sketch of Fuller's life can be
found in G. P. Hamilton, *Beacon Lights of the Race* (Memphis, 1911),
185–204. See also Rayford W. Logan, "Thomas Oscar Fuller," in *Dictionary of American Negro Biography,* ed. Rayford W. Logan and
Michael R. Winston (New York, 1982), 248–49.

2. Fuller, *Twenty Years,* 15; Frenise A. Logan, *The Negro in
North Carolina, 1876–1894* (Chapel Hill, N.C., 1964), 145.

3. J. A. Whitted, *A History of the Negro Baptists in North Carolina* (Raleigh, N.C., 1918), 19–20. Shaw University received financial
support from the American Baptist Home Mission Society, the same
organization that helped to support Howe Institute.

4. Fuller, *Twenty Years,* 16–18.

5. Ibid., 199, 291; W. E. B. Dubois, *The College-Bred Negro
American* (Atlanta, 1910), 45.

6. Fuller, *Twenty Years,* 25–28, 31–32.

7. Rufus E. Clement, "A History of Negro Education in North
Carolina, 1865–1928" (Ph.D. diss., Northwestern University, 1930),
167. For additional information about the state of black education in
North Carolina, see Hugh Victor Brown, *A History of the Education
of Negroes in North Carolina* (Raleigh, N.C., 1961), 27.

8. *Warrenton Gazette,* 22 September 1894.

9. Fuller, *Twenty Years,* 37–38.

10. Hugh T. Lefler and Albert R. Newsome, *The History of a
Southern State, North Carolina* (Chapel Hill, N.C., 1973), 552–56;
Twenty Years, 40, 44.

11. Fuller, *Twenty Years,* 58, 107–10.

12. *Memphis Commercial Appeal,* 30 March 1901; Hamilton,
Beacon Lights, 188. Fuller believed that teaching the ministerial class
served "as an introduction for me, as to ability and scholarship." See
Fuller, *Twenty Years,* 116.

13. Fuller, *Twenty Years,* 117. Italics in the original.

14. *Catalogue of Howe Collegiate Institute, Session 1912–1913,* 9; Fuller, *Twenty Years,* 115–116. For additional insights into the creation of Howe Institute, see Ruth Marie Powell, "A History of Negro Educational Institutions Sponsored by the Baptists of Tennessee from 1864–1934" (M.S. thesis, Tennessee A and I University, 1954).

15. *Catalogue of Howe Collegiate Institute,* 9; Hamilton, *Beacon Lights,* 191; Fuller, *Twenty Years,* 115; Thomas Jesse Jones, ed., *Negro Education: A Study of the Private and Higher Schools for Colored People in the United States,* 2 vols., (Washington, D.C., 1917), 2: 558. Kortrecht High School, the only public high school for black students, was founded in 1890. LeMoyne Institute, an elementary-secondary school with an emphasis upon normal school training, was founded by the American Missionary Associates in 1869.

16. U.S. Department of the Interior, Census Office, *Ninth Census of the United States, 1870: Population,* (Washington, 1872) 1:268; U.S. Department of the Interior, Census Office, *Twelfth Census of the United States, 1900: Population* (Washington, 1902) 1: 642. There were 49,910 blacks and 52,380 whites living in Memphis in 1900. The five cities that had larger black populations than Memphis in 1900 were, in descending order: Washington, D.C., Baltimore, New Orleans, Philadelphia, and New York City. See U.S. Department of Commerce, Bureau of Census, *Negro Population, 1790–1915* (Washington, D.C., 1918), 93. For an account of the black migration to Memphis see William D. Miller, *Memphis during the Progressive Era, 1900–1917* (Memphis, 1957), 7.

17. Lester C. Lamon, "Negroes in Tennessee, 1900–1930" (Ph.D. diss., University of North Carolina, 1971), 178; David M. Tucker, *Black Pastors and Leaders: Memphis, 1819–1972* (Memphis, 1975), 7, 10.

18. Fuller's speech to local black clergymen in 1908 is cited in W. N. Hartshorn, ed., *An Era of Progress and Promise, 1863–1910: The Religious, Moral, and Educational Development of the American Negro since his Emancipation* (Boston, 1910), 117. Fuller's business dealings are well documented in Hamilton, *Beacon Lights,* 202.

19. Hamilton, *Beacon Lights,* 202–3.

20. Miller, *Memphis,* 19. For more pertinent insights into the racial climate of Tennessee, see David M. Tucker, *Lieutenant Lee of Beale Street* (Nashville, 1971), 14; Lamon, "Negroes in Tennessee," 59; and Cynthia G. Fleming, "The Development of Black Education in Tennessee, 1865–1920" (Ph.D. diss., Duke University, 1977), 148–49. The target of the 1901 legislation was the Presbyterian-supported Maryville College in Maryville, where a black woman taught white students.

21. *Memphis Commercial Appeal,* 18 June 1900, 10 August 1901, 22 October 1901, and 17 March 1902.

22. Lamon, "Negroes in Tennessee," 46; *Memphis Commercial Appeal,* 7 March 1905.

23. *Memphis Commercial Appeal,* 3 July 1905.

24. Fuller, *Twenty Years,* 27, 95, 159, 193.
25. Tucker, *Black Pastors and Leaders,* 55; Lamon, "Negroes in Tennessee," 55–56.
26. Hartshorn, *An Era of Progress,* 117.
27. *The Baptist Home Mission Monthly* 26 (October 1904): 73; *Memphis Commercial Appeal,* 18 October 1905; Jones, *Negro Education* 2:559.
28. Data on the rural origins of the student body was derived from a study of class lists found in the *Catalogue of Howe Collegiate Institute,* 1912–1913; Jones, *Negro Education* 2:558.
29. Fuller, *Twenty Years,* 209, 228.
30. *Catalogue of Howe Collegiate Institute,* 1912–1913, 12, 14, 54.
31. Fuller, *Twenty Years,* 171.
32. *Memphis Commercial Appeal,* 5 December 1909; *Catalogue of Howe Collegiate Institute,* 1912–1913, 12, 54.
33. *Catalogue of Howe Collegiate Institute,* 1912–1913, 15; *Memphis Commercial Appeal,* 5 December 1909.
34. *Memphis Commercial Appeal,* 5 December 1909; *Catalogue of Howe Collegiate Institute,* 1912–1913, 35–37.
35. *Catalogue of Howe Collegiate Institute,* 1912–1913, 35–43.
36. *Memphis Commercial Appeal,* 5 December 1909.
37. Booker T. Washington, *Up from Slavery* (New York, 1901; reprint, Garden City, N.Y., 1929), 88.
38. *The Baptist Home Mission Monthly* 26 (October 1904): 73.
39. *Memphis Commercial Appeal,* 5 December 1909.
40. Ibid.
41. Fuller, *Twenty Years,* 229; *Memphis Commercial Appeal,* 18 October 1905; Jones, *Negro Education* 2:559.
42. *Catalogue of Howe Collegiate Institute,* 11–19. Only 37 percent of the student body at Howe in 1913 was enrolled in manual training.
43. Tucker, *Black Pastors and Leaders,* 60–66; August Meier, *Negro Thought in America, 1880–1915: Racial Ideologies in the Age of Booker T. Washington* (Ann Arbor, Mich., 1963), 93.
44. *Memphis Commercial Appeal,* 18 October 1905; Jones, *Negro Education* 2:559; G. P. Hamilton, *The Bright Side of Memphis* (Memphis, 1908), 254. Faculty members of Howe in 1908 were graduates of such church-related schools as LeMoyne Institute (Memphis), affiliated with the Congregational Church, Walden University (Nashville), operated by the Methodist Episcopal Church and Geneva College (Pa.), established by the Reformed Presbyterian Church of North America.
45. Thomas O. Fuller, "Bible Training at Howe Institute," *The Baptist Home Mission Monthly* 26 (June 1904): 232.
46. *Catalogue of Howe Collegiate Institute,* 19–20; *Memphis Commercial Appeal,* 5 December 1909; Fuller, *Twenty Years,* 131, 172.
47. Fuller, *Twenty Years,* 172.

48. *Catalogue of Howe Collegiate Institute,* 1912–1913, 19; Fuller, *Twenty Years,* 112–13.

49. *Catalogue of Howe Collegiate Institute,* 1912–1913, 9; Fuller, *Twenty Years,* 116.

50. *Memphis Commercial Appeal,* 18 October 1905; *Minutes of the Tennessee Missionary and Education Convention,* 1906, 20. A concise history of the involvement of the ABHMS in black education can be found in James M. McPherson, *The Abolitionist Legacy from Reconstruction to the NAACP* (Princeton, 1975), 144, 412–13.

51. R. R. Wright, Sr., *Self-Help in Negro Education* (Cheyney, Pa., 1912), 13; *Memphis Commercial Appeal,* 5 December 1909. It was possible that the ABHMS donated $620 for 1909–10 and that this support accounted for the difference between the money raised by black supporters and the total school budget. By 1915 the ABHMS was contributing $820 to Howe Institute, with tuition accounting for 56 percent of the school's income. See Jones, *Negro Education* 2:559.

52. Fuller, *Twenty Years,* 129, 137, 153; *Catalogue of Howe Collegiate Institute,* 1912–13, 11.

53. Fuller, *Twenty Years,* 125, 155, 168–69, 171; *Memphis Commercial Appeal,* 5 December 1909.

54. Hamilton, *Beacon Lights,* 193, 195; Hamilton, *The Bright Side of Memphis,* 140.

55. Hamilton, *Beacon Lights,* 191.

56. Hamilton, *The Bright Side of Memphis,* 141; Tucker, *Black Pastors and Leaders,* 61; *Memphis Commercial Appeal,* 5 December 1909.

57. Fuller, *Twenty Years,* 191, 242, 159.

Chapter Six

1. William J. Edwards, *Twenty-Five Years in the Black Belt* (Boston, 1918), 135.

2. Thomas O. Fuller, *Twenty Years in Public Life, 1890–1910* (Nashville, 1910), 106, 188–91.

3. August Meier, "Negro Class Structure and Ideology in the Age of Booker T. Washington," *Phylon* 23 (Fall 1962): 258.

4. C. Vann Woodward, *The Strange Career of Jim Crow* (New York, 1955), 71.

5. Booker T. Washington to William J. Edwards, 30 November 1914, Booker T. Washington Papers, Manuscripts Division, Library of Congress (hereafter cited as BTW Papers).

6. John R. Webster, *A Brief Historical Sketch of the Early Days of the Piney Woods School* (Piney Woods, Miss., n.d.), 19; Alferdteen Harrison, *Piney Woods School: An Oral History* (Jackson, Miss., 1982), 115.

7. Leola Hughes, interview by Alferdteen Harrison, 5 September

1978, OHO1.4b, transcript, Oral History Study of Black Educational Institutions in Mississippi, Jackson State University, Oral History Program, Jackson, Miss.

8. Quoted in David M. Tucker, *Black Pastors and Leaders: Memphis, 1819–1972* (Memphis, 1975), 61.

9. Ibid., 60–61.

10. Webster, *A Brief Historical Sketch,* 20.

11. Booker T. Washington, *Up from Slavery* (New York, 1901; reprint, Garden City, N.Y., 1929), 81.

12. Fuller, *Twenty Years,* 228, 238.

13. Sandra Kissick, "The Theme of Exodus Versus Permanence in the South in Negro Autobiographies Published Between 1900 and 1915" (Ph.D. diss., University of Michigan, 1972), 178, 186.

14. Edwards, *Twenty-Five Years,* 51; William H. Holtzclaw, *The Black Man's Burden* (New York, 1915), 227–28.

15. Laurence C. Jones, *Up through Difficulties* (n.p., 1913), 77–79; Fuller, *Twenty Years,* 221.

16. Gutman is cited in James D. Anderson, "Ex-Slaves and the Rise of Universal Education in the New South, 1860–1880," in *Education and the Rise of the New South,* ed. Ronald K. Goodenow and Arthur O. White (Boston, 1981), 2–4.

17. James D. Anderson, "Education for Servitude: The Social Purposes of Schooling in the Black South, 1870–1930" (Ph.D. diss., University of Illinois at Urbana-Champaign, 1973); Donald Spivey, *Schooling for the New Slavery: Black Industrial Education, 1868–1915* (Westport, Conn., 1978).

Bibliography

Primary Sources

Manuscripts

Carver, George Washington. Papers. Microfilm Edition. Tuskegee Institute Archives, Tuskegee University, Alabama.

Jones, Laurence C. Alumni Vertical Information Folder. University of Iowa Archives, Iowa City, Iowa.

Macbride, Thomas H. Papers. University of Iowa Archives, Iowa City, Ia.

Peabody Education Fund Papers. Special Collection, The Jean and Alexander Heard Library, Vanderbilt University, Nashville, Tennessee.

Records of the Snow Hill Institute, 1899–1958. Microfilm Edition. Talladega College Historical Collections, Talladega, Alabama.

Stokes, J. G. Phelps. Papers. Rare Book and Manuscript Library, Columbia University, New York City.

Villard, Oscar Garrison. Papers. Houghton Library, Harvard University, Cambridge, Mass.

Washington, Booker T. Papers. Manuscripts Division, Library of Congress, Washington, D.C.

Official Records and Documents

PUBLICATIONS OF THE UNITED STATES GOVERNMENT

Jones, Thomas Jesse, ed. *Negro Education: A Study of the Private and Higher Schools for Colored People in the United States.* 2 vols. Washington, D.C., 1917.

U.S. Bureau of Education. *Report of the Commissioner of Education, 1881–1916.*

U.S. Bureau of Labor. *Seventeenth Annual Report of the Commissioner of Labor, 1902.*

_____. *Twenty-Fifth Annual Report of the Commissioner of Labor, 1910.*

U.S. Department of Commerce. Bureau of Census. *Negro Population, 1790–1915.* Washington, D.C., 1918.
U.S. Department of the Interior. Census Office. *Ninth Census of the United States, 1870: Population,* Vol. 1.
U.S. Department of the Interior. Census Office. *Eleventh Census of the United States, 1890: Population.* Vol. 1.
_____. Census Office. *Twelfth Census of the United States, 1900: Population.* Vol. 1.
_____. Census Office. *Thirteenth Census of the United States, 1910: Population.* Vol. 2.
Weeks, Stephen B. *The History of Public School Education in Alabama.* Bureau of Education, Bulletin No. 12, 1915. Washington, D.C., 1915.

CATALOGS, DIRECTORIES, DOCUMENTS, REPORTS, AND PROCEEDINGS

The Alumni Directory of the University of Iowa, 1911. Iowa City, Ia.: University of Iowa Alumni Publications, 1911.
The Alumni Directory of the Iowa Law School, 1866–1961. Iowa City, Ia.: University of Iowa College of Law, 1961.
Proceedings and Reports of the John F. Slater Fund for Year Ending September 30, 1916. New York, 1916.

SNOW HILL INSTITUTE

Fifth Annual Catalogue of the Snow Hill Normal and Industrial Institute, 1898–99.
Fifth Annual Report of the Principal [of Snow Hill Institute], 10 May 1899.
Eighth Annual Catalogue of the Snow Hill Normal and Industrial Institute, 1901–2.
Tenth Annual Catalogue of the Snow Hill Normal and Industrial Institute, 1903–4.
Tenth Annual Report of the Principal and Treasurer of the Snow Hill Normal and Industrial Institute, 5 May 1904.
Eleventh Annual Report of the Principal and Treasurer of the Snow Hill Normal and Industrial Institute, 1905.
Fourteenth Annual Catalogue of the Snow Hill Normal and Industrial Institute, 1907–8.
Edwards, William J. "Some Results of the Snow Hill Normal and Industrial Institute, 1894–1910." N.p., n.d.
Seventeenth Annual Catalogue of the Snow Hill Normal and Industrial Institute, 1911–12.
Eighteenth Annual Report of the Principal and Treasurer of the Snow Hill Normal and Industrial Institute, 1911–12.
Twenty-Seventh Annual Catalogue of Snow Hill Normal and Industrial Institute, 1920–21.

UTICA INSTITUTE

Fifth Annual Statement of the Principal and Treasurer of the Utica Normal and Industrial Institute, for the Year Ending May 2, 1907.
Fifth Annual Financial Statement of the Principal and Treasurer of the Utica, Mississippi, Normal and Industrial Institute, for the Year Ending May 4, 1908.
Sixth Annual Financial Statement of the Principal and Treasurer of the Utica, Mississippi, Normal and Industrial Institute, for the Year Ending May 4, 1909.
Seventh Annual Financial Statement of the Principal and Treasurer of the Utica, Mississippi, Normal and Industrial Institute, for the Year Ending June 1, 1910.
Report of the Principal and Treasurer of the Utica Normal and Industrial [sic] Institute, for the Year Ending June 1, 1912.
Report of the Principal and Treasurer of the Utica Normal and Industrial Institute, for the Year Ending June 1, 1913.
Annual Report Edition of the Principal and Treasurer, Utica Institute, 1914.
Charter of Incorporation of the Utica Normal and Industrial Institute, 13 January 1903. Office of Secretary of State, Jackson, Miss.

THE PINEY WOODS SCHOOL

Charter of Incorporation of the Piney Woods Country Life School, 17 May 1913. Office of Secretary of State, Jackson, Miss.

HOWE INSTITUTE

The Baptist Home Mission Monthly, 1904.
Catalogue of Howe Collegiate Institute, Session 1912–1913.
Minutes of the Tennessee Baptist Missionary and Education Convention, 1906.

NEWSPAPERS

Brandon [Miss.] *News,* 30 January 1913.
Des Moines Iowa State Bystander, 1899–1913.
Des Moines Register and Leader, 1909–13.
Jackson [Miss.] *Daily News,* 1903–15.
Marshalltown [Ia.] *Times-Republican,* 1899–1903.
Memphis Commercial Appeal, 1900–1910; 22 June 1942.
Warrenton [N.C.] *Gazette,* 1894–1900.

SCHOOL NEWSPAPERS AND NEWSLETTERS

The Black Belt, July 1899, August 1902.
Daily Iowan, 1903–7.

The Pine Torch, 1911–14.
Southern Notes, September 1906, May 1908, May 1911, January 1915.

ORAL HISTORY TRANSCRIPTS

Bass, Nellie. Interview by Alferdteen Harrison, 24 February 1974.
Transcript, Oral History Study of Black Educational Institutions
in Mississippi, Jackson State University Oral History Program,
Jackson, Miss.
Hughes, Leola. Interview by Alferdteen Harrison, 5 September 1978.
Transcript, Oral History Study of Black Educational Institutions
in Mississippi, Jackson State University Oral History Program,
Jackson, Miss.
Jones, Laurence C. Interview by Alferdteen Harrison, 25 February
1974. Transcript, Oral History Study of Black Educational Institu-
tions in Mississippi, Jackson State University Oral History Pro-
gram, Jackson, Miss.
Weathersby, Eva. Interview by Alferdteen Harrison, 27 June 1973.
Transcript, Oral History Study of Black Educational Institutions
in Mississippi, Jackson State University Oral History Program,
Jackson, Miss.

ARTICLES

Alexander, Charles. "Tuskegee Graduates and Their Achievements."
Alexander's Magazine 2 (May 1906): 94–104.
_____. "Snow Hill Normal and Industrial Institute." *Alexander's Mag-
azine* 3 (December 1906): 66–68.
_____. "Down in Mississippi." *Alexander's Magazine* 7 (February
1909): 177–82.
Dickerman, G. S. "From Iowa to Mississippi." *The Crisis* 6 (July 1913):
137–40.
Edwards, William J. "Uplifting the Submerged Masses." In *Tuskegee
and Its People: Their Ideals and Achievements,* edited by Booker
T. Washington, 224–52. New York, 1905. Reprint. New York,
1969.
Fuller, Thomas O. "Bible Training at Howe Institute." *The Baptist
Home Mission Monthly* 26 (June 1904): 232.
Holtzclaw, William H. "A School Principal's Story." In *Tuskegee and
Its People: Their Ideals and Achievements,* edited by Booker T.
Washington, 111–40. New York, 1905. Reprint. New York, 1969.
_____. "A Negro's Life Story." *World's Work* 12 (September 1906):
7988–93.
Jones, Laurence C. "Piney Woods School." *Southern Workman* 60
(June 1931): 20–23.
Kealing, H. T. "Booker T. Washington's Tour through Mississippi: A

New Form of University Extension." *Alexander's Magazine* 7 (November 1908): 34–37.

Penney, Emma C. "A Light in the Black Belt of Mississippi." *Alexander's Magazine* 5 (November 1907): 25–27.

Pickens, William. "The Talladega Letter on Snow Hill." *Alexander's Magazine* 2 (May 1906): 18.

_____. "Utica." *The Independent* 72 (February 1912): 405–7.

Slatter, H. D. "Noble Work in the Black Belt." *Alexander's Magazine* 1 (May 1905): 19–20.

"Speech of William J. Edwards." *Alexander's Magazine* 2 (May 1906): 63–65.

Washington, Booker T. "Signs of Progress among the Negroes." *Century Magazine* 59 (January 1900): 472–78.

_____. "A Man About Whom the World Should Know." *The Independent* 58 (May 1905): 1115–16.

_____. "A Cheerful Journey through Mississippi." *World's Work* 17 (February 1909): 11278–82.

GENERAL WORKS

Dubois, W. E. B. *The Souls of Black Folk.* Chicago, 1903. Reprint. New York, 1968.

_____. *The College-Bred Negro American.* Atlanta, 1910.

Edwards, William J. *Twenty-Five Years in the Black Belt.* Boston, 1918.

Fuller, Thomas O. *Twenty Years in Public Life, 1890–1910.* Nashville, 1910.

Hamilton, G. P. *The Bright Side of Memphis.* Memphis, 1908.

_____. *Beacon Lights of the Race.* Memphis, 1911.

Harlan, Louis R., et al., eds. *The Booker T. Washington Papers.* 13 vols. Urbana, Ill., 1972–84.

Hartshorn, W. N., ed. *An Era of Progress and Promise, 1863–1910: The Religious, Moral, and Educational Development of the American Negro since his Emancipation.* Boston, 1910.

Holtzclaw, William H. *The Black Man's Burden.* New York, 1915.

Jones, Laurence C. *Up through Difficulties.* n. p. 1913.

_____. *Piney Woods and its Story.* New York, 1913.

Scott, Emmett Jay, and Stowe, Lyman Beecher. *Booker T. Washington: Builder of a Civilization.* Garden City, N. Y., 1918.

Thirty Years of Lynching in the United States, 1889–1918. New York, 1919.

Washington, Booker T. *Up from Slavery.* New York, 1901. Reprint. Garden City, N. Y., 1929.

_____., ed. *Tuskegee and Its People: Their Ideals and Achievements.* New York, 1905. Reprint. New York, 1969.

Webster, John R. *A Brief Historical Sketch of the Early Days of the*

Piney Woods School. Piney Woods, Miss., n.d.

Work, Monroe Nathan. *Industrial Work of Tuskegee Graduates and Former Students during the Year 1910.* Tuskegee Institute, Ala., 1911.

Wright, R. R., Sr. *Self-Help in Negro Education.* Cheyney, Pa., 1912.

Secondary Sources

Articles

Bergmann, Leola N. "The Negro in Iowa." *The Iowa Journal of History and Politics* 46 (January 1948): 3–90.

Browning, Jane E. Smith, and Williams, John B. "History and Goals of Black Institutions of Higher Learning." In *Black Colleges in America,* edited by Charles V. Willie and Ronald R. Edmonds, 68–89. New York, 1978.

Enck, Henry S. "Black Self-Help in the Progressive Era: The 'Northern Campaigns' of Smaller Southern Black Industrial Schools 1900–1915." *Journal of Negro History* 61 (January 1976): 73–87.

Friedman, Lawrence J. "The Search for Docility: Racial Thought in the White South, 1861–1917." *Phylon* 31 (Fall 1970): 313–23.

Gavins, Raymond. "Gordon Blaine Hancock: A Black Profile from the New South." *Journal of Negro History* 59 (July 1974): 207–27.

Gershenberg, Irving. "The Negro and the Development of White Public Education in the South: Alabama, 1880–1930." *Journal of Negro Education* 39 (Winter 1970): 50–59.

Martin, William H. "Unique Contributions of Negro Educators." In *Negro Education in America,* edited by Virgil A. Clift, et al., 60–92. New York, 1962.

Meier, August. "The Beginning of Industrial Education in Negro Schools." *The Midwest Journal* 7 (Spring 1955): 21–44.

_____. "The Vogue of Industrial Education." *The Midwest Journal* 7 (Fall 1955): 241–66.

_____. "Negro Class Structure and Ideology in the Age of Booker T. Washington." *Phylon* 23 (Fall 1962): 258–66.

Savage, W. Sherman. "The Legal Provisions for Negro Schools in Missouri from 1865 to 1890." *Journal of Negro History* 16 (July 1931): 309–21.

Sisk, Glen. "The Educational Awakening in Alabama and its Effect upon the Black Belt, 1900–1917." *Journal of Negro Education* 25 (Spring 1956): 191–96.

White, Eugene E. "Anti-Racial Agitation in Politics: James Kimble Vardaman in the Mississippi Gubernatorial Campaign of 1903." *Journal of Mississippi History* 7 (April 1945): 91–110.

Wright, Stephen J. "The Development of the Hampton-Tuskegee Pattern of Higher Education." *Phylon* 10 (December 1950): 334–42.

General Works

Anderson, Eric. *Race and Politics in North Carolina, 1872–1901.* Baton Rouge, La., 1981.

Aurner, Clarence R. *History of Education in Iowa.* 4 vols. Iowa City, 1914–16.

Bailey, Hugh C. *Liberalism in the New South: Social Reformers and the Progressive Movement.* Coral Gables, Fla., 1969.

Batlin, William, and Moscrip, F. A. *Past and Present of Marshall County, Iowa.* Indianapolis, 1912.

Bond, Horace Mann. *The Education of the Negro in the American Social Order.* New York, 1934.

———. *Negro Education in Alabama: A Study in Cotton and Steel.* Washington, D.C., 1939.

Brawley, Benjamin. *Early Efforts for Industrial Education.* New York, 1923.

Brown, Hugh Victor. *A History of the Education of Negroes in North Carolina.* Raleigh, N.C., 1961.

Bullock, Henry Allen. *A History of Negro Education in the South from 1619 to the Present.* Cambridge, 1967.

Day, Beth. *The Little Professor of Piney Woods: The Story of Laurence Jones.* New York, 1955.

Edmonds, Helen G. *The Negro and Fusion Politics in North Carolina, 1894–1901.* Chapel Hill, N.C., 1951.

Fredrickson, George M. *The Black Image in the White Mind: The Debate on Afro-American Character and Destiny, 1817–1914.* New York, 1971.

Friedman, Lawrence J. *The White Savage: Racial Fantasies in the Post-bellum South.* Englewood Cliffs, N.J., 1970.

Goodenow, Ronald, and White, Arthur O., eds. *Education and the Rise of the New South.* Boston, 1981.

Greene, Lorenzo J., Kremer, Gary R., and Holland, Anthony P. *Missouri's Black Heritage.* St. Louis, 1980.

Harlan, Louis R. *Booker T. Washington: The Making of a Black Leader, 1856–1901.* New York, 1972.

———. *Booker T. Washington: The Wizard of Tuskegee, 1901–1915.* New York, 1983.

Harrison, Alferdteen B. *Piney Woods School: An Oral History.* Jackson, Miss., 1982.

Holtzclaw, R. Fulton. *William Henry Holtzclaw: Scholar in Ebony.* Cleveland, 1977.

Jacoway, Elizabeth. *Yankee Missionaries in the South: The Penn School Experiment.* Baton Rouge, La., 1980.

Kellogg, Charles F. *NAACP.* Baltimore, 1967.

Kirwan, Albert D. *Revolt of the Rednecks: Mississippi Politics, 1876–1925.* Lexington, Ky., 1951.

Larrie, Reginald R. *Makin' Free: African-Americans in the Northwest Territory.* Detroit, 1981.

Leavell, Ullin W. *Philanthropy in Negro Education.* Nashville, 1930.

Lefler, Hugh T., and Newsome, Albert R. *The History of a Southern State, North Carolina.* Chapel Hill, N. C. 1973.

Logan, Frenise A. *The Negro in North Carolina, 1876–1894.* Chapel Hill, N.C., 1964.

Logan, Rayford W., and Winston, Michael R., eds. *Dictionary of American Negro Biography.* New York, 1982.

McLemore, Richard A. *A History of Mississippi.* 2 vols. Hattiesburg, Miss., 1973.

McPherson, James M. *The Abolitionist Legacy from Reconstruction to the NAACP.* Princeton, 1975.

Mathews, Basil. *Booker T. Washington: Educator and Interracial Interpreter.* Cambridge, 1948.

Meier, August. *Negro Thought in Ameria, 1880–1915: Racial Ideologies in the Age of Booker T. Washington.* Ann Arbor, Mich., 1963.

Miller, William D. *Memphis during the Progressive Era, 1900–1917.* Memphis, 1957.

Moorman, J. H., and Barrett, E. C., eds. *Leaders of the Colored Race in Alabama.* Mobile, Ala., 1928.

Mott, Frank Luther. *A History of American Magazines.* 5 vols. Cambridge, 1938–68.

Noble, Stuart Grayson. *Forty Years of the Public Schools in Mississippi.* New York, 1918.

Prather, H. Leon, Jr. *Resurgent Politics and Educational Progressivism in the New South: North Carolina, 1890–1913.* Rutherford, N. J., 1979.

Purcell, Leslie Harper. *Miracle in Mississippi: Laurence C. Jones of Piney Woods.* New York, 1956.

Richardson, Clement, ed. *The National Cyclopedia of the Colored Race.* Montgomery, Ala., 1919.

Sewell, George A. *Mississippi Black History Makers.* Jackson, Miss., 1977.

Sherer, Robert G. *Subordination or Liberation?: The Development and Conflicting Theories of Black Education in Nineteenth Century Alabama.* University, Ala., 1977.

Spivey, Donald. *Schooling for the New Slavery: Black Industrial Education, 1868–1915.* Westport, Conn., 1978.

Stokes, Anson Phelps. *Tuskegee Institute: The First Fifty Years.* Tuskegee, Ala., 1931.

Tucker, David M. *Lieutenant Lee of Beale Street.* Nashville, 1971.

_____. *Black Pastors and Leaders: Memphis, 1819–1972.* Memphis, 1975.

Tyms, James D. *The Rise of Religious Education among Negro Baptists.* New York, 1965.

West, Earl H. *The Black American and Education.* Columbus, Ohio, 1972.
Whitted, J. A. *A History of the Negro Baptists in North Carolina.* Raleigh, N.C., 1918.
Woodward, C. Vann. *Origins of the New South, 1877–1913.* Baton Rouge, La., 1951.
_____.*The Strange Career of Jim Crow.* New York, 1955.

Dissertations

Anderson, James D. "Education for Servitude: The Social Purposes of Schooling in the Black South, 1870–1930." Ph.D. diss., University of Illinois at Urbana-Champaign, 1973.
Citro, Joseph F. "Booker T. Washington's Tuskegee Institute: Black School-Community, 1900–1915." Ed.D. diss., University of Rochester, 1973.
Clement, Rufus E. "A History of Negro Education in North Carolina, 1865–1928." Ph.D. diss., Northwestern University, 1930.
Cobbins, Sam. "Industrial Education for Black Americans in Mississippi, 1862–1965." Ed.D. diss., Mississippi State University, 1975.
Davis, Joseph. "A Historical Study of Snow Hill Normal and Industrial Institute and its Contribution to the Educational Program of the State of Alabama." M.Ed. thesis, Alabama State University, 1954.
Enck, Henry Snyder. "The Burden Borne: Northern White Philanthropy and Southern Black Industrial Education, 1900–1915." Ph.D. diss., University of Cincinnati, 1970.
Fleming, Cynthia G. "The Development of Black Education in Tennessee, 1865–1920." Ph.D. diss., Duke University, 1977.
Kissick, Sandra. "The Theme of Exodus Versus Permanence in the South in Negro Autobiographies Published Between 1900 and 1915." Ph.D. diss., University of Michigan, 1972.
Lamon, Lester C. "Negroes in Tennessee, 1900–1930." Ph.D diss., University of North Carolina, 1971.
Powell, Ruth Marie. "A History of Negro Educational Institutions Sponsored by the Baptists of Tennessee from 1864–1934." M.S. thesis, Tennessee A and I University, 1954.
Washington, Walter. "Utica Junior College, 1903–1957: A Half-Century of Education for Negroes." Ed.D. diss., University of Southern Mississippi, 1970.

Index

119